John Waller

PERMANENT DRIFT

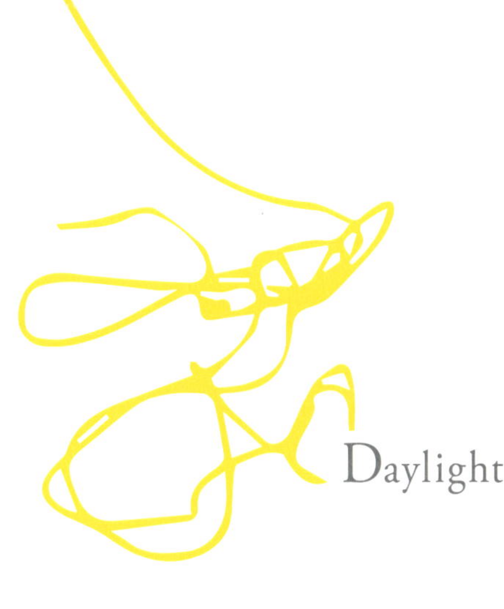

Daylight

Cofounders: Taj Forer and Michael Itkoff
Creative Director: Ursula Damm
Copy Editor: Gabrielle Fastman

ISBN: 978-1-942084-96-9

Printed by Ofset Yapımevi, Turkey

Daylight Books
E-mail: info@daylightbooks.org
Web: www.daylightbooks.org

"The 'new towns' of the technological pseudo-peasantry are the clearest of indications, inscribed on the land, of the break with historical time on which they are founded; their motto might well be: 'On this spot, nothing will ever happen—*and nothing ever has*.'"

—Guy Debord, "Environmental Planning"

"Move out!"

—Anonymous motorist, shouted from a passing car

Foreword

When I briefly lived in Olde Kensington, a post-industrial area of Philadelphia, the neighborhood underwent a major development push. You could call it gentrification, and I wouldn't argue with you.

As a lone walker, muddling my way through this unfamiliar and transitional neighborhood, I set out to document my time in Olde Kensington. The sense that some invisible force seemed to be directing these walks, influencing my movements in secret, was hard to ignore. This reticent escort seemed intent on eliciting conflicting senses of adversity, apprehension, desire, and elation.

As a record of these ambulations, the photographs in this book limn the tension between the extant and the imminent, the intervallic experience of living in a city in flux, and a complicated relationship to place.

—John Waller

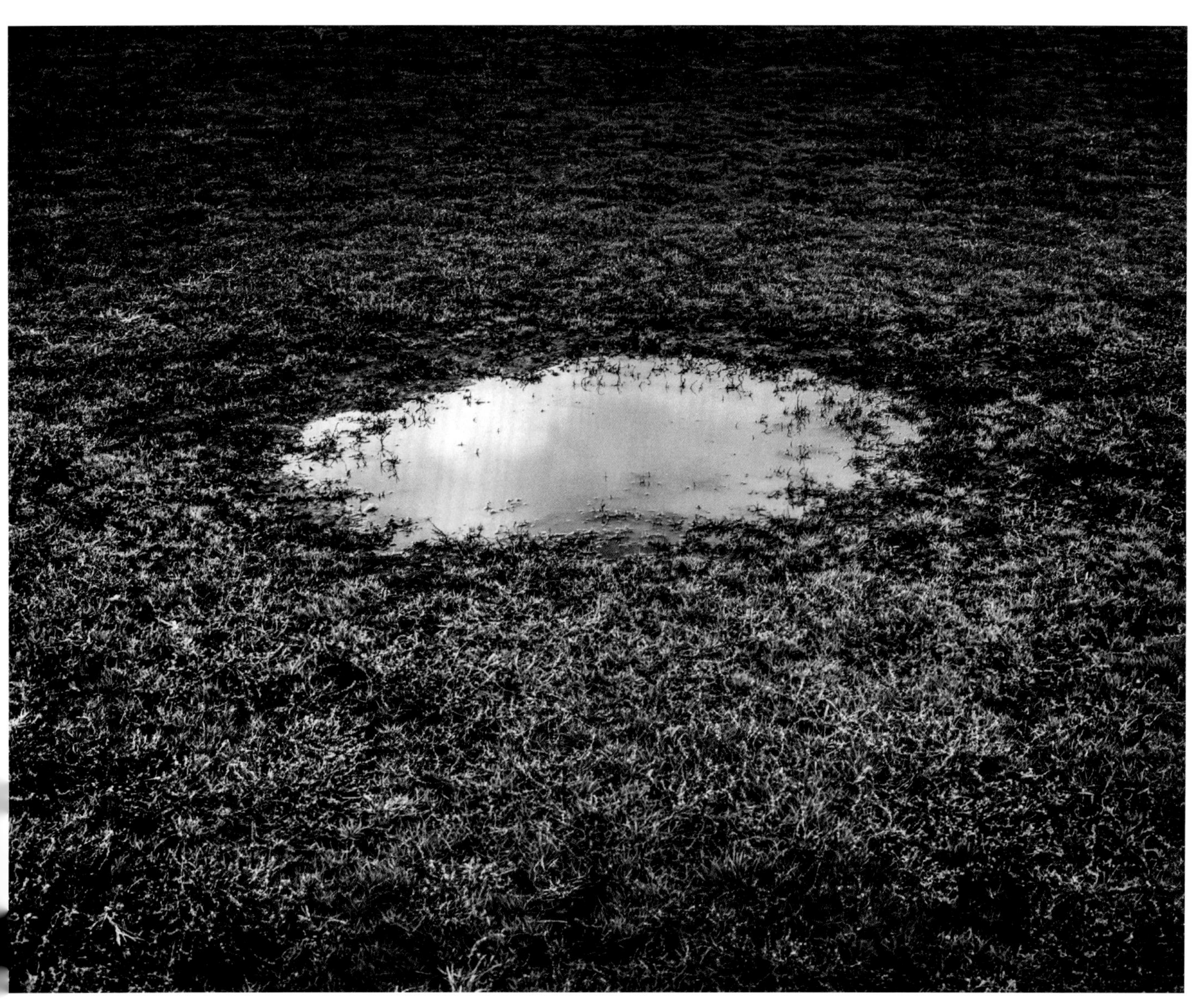

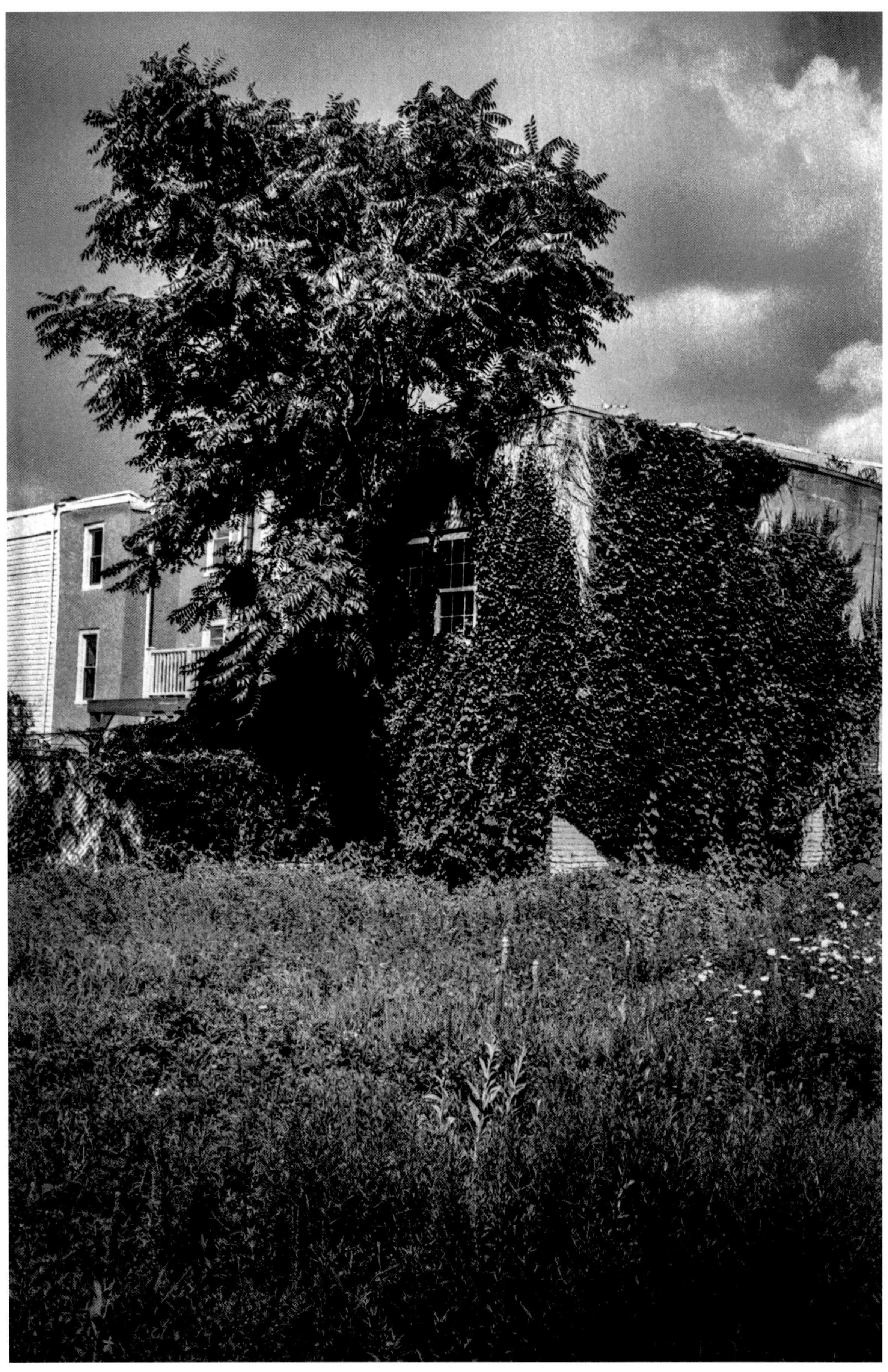

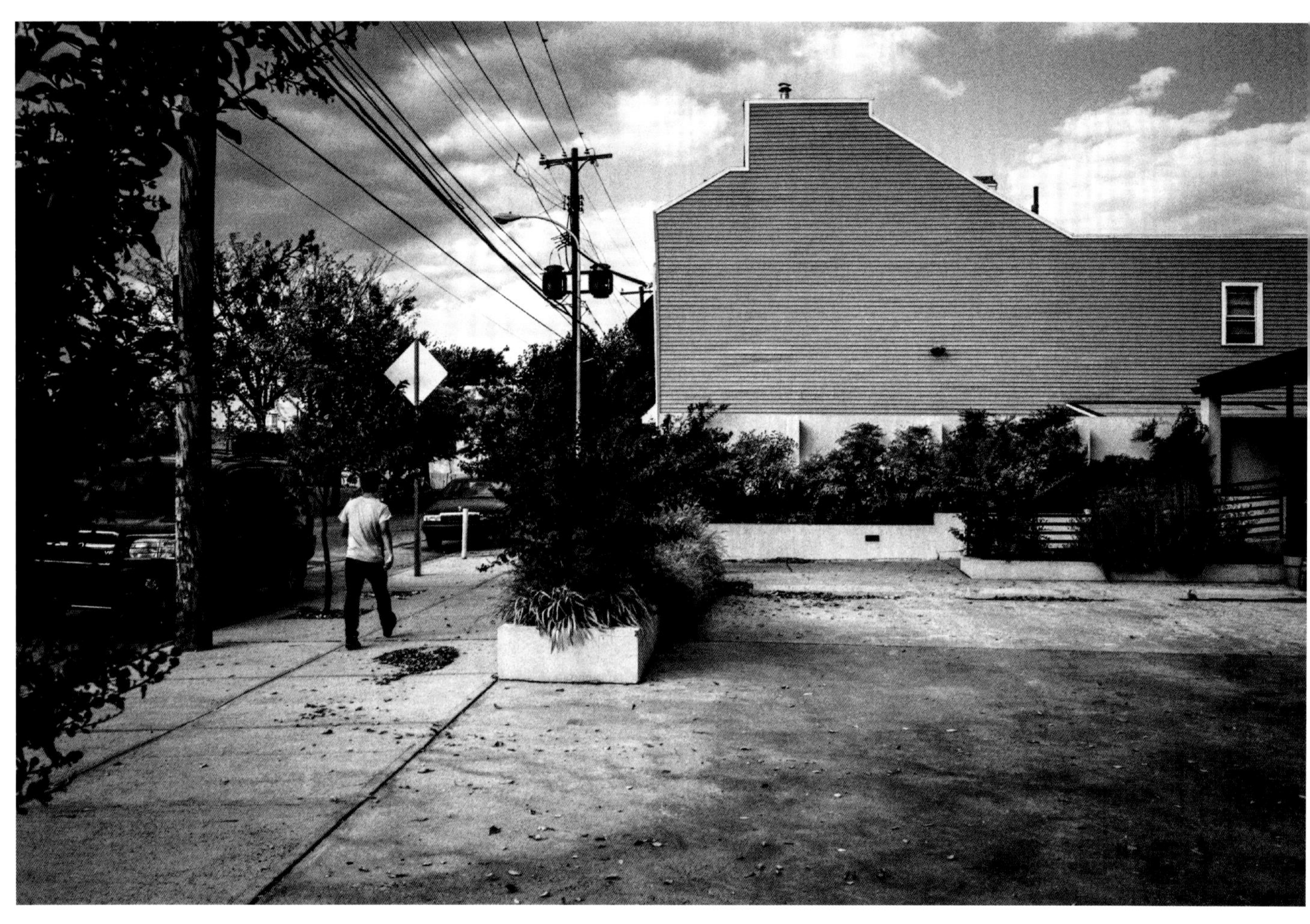

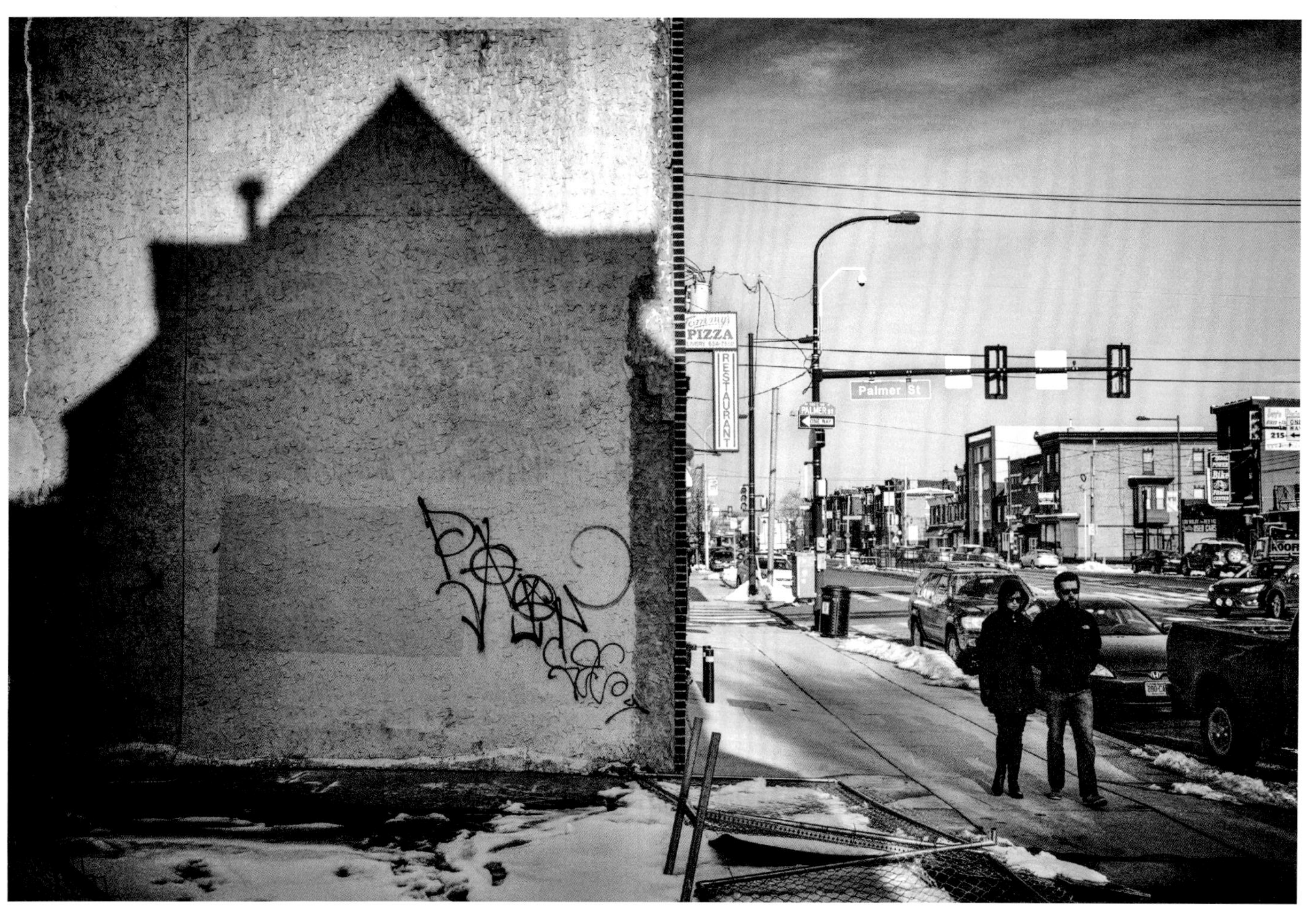

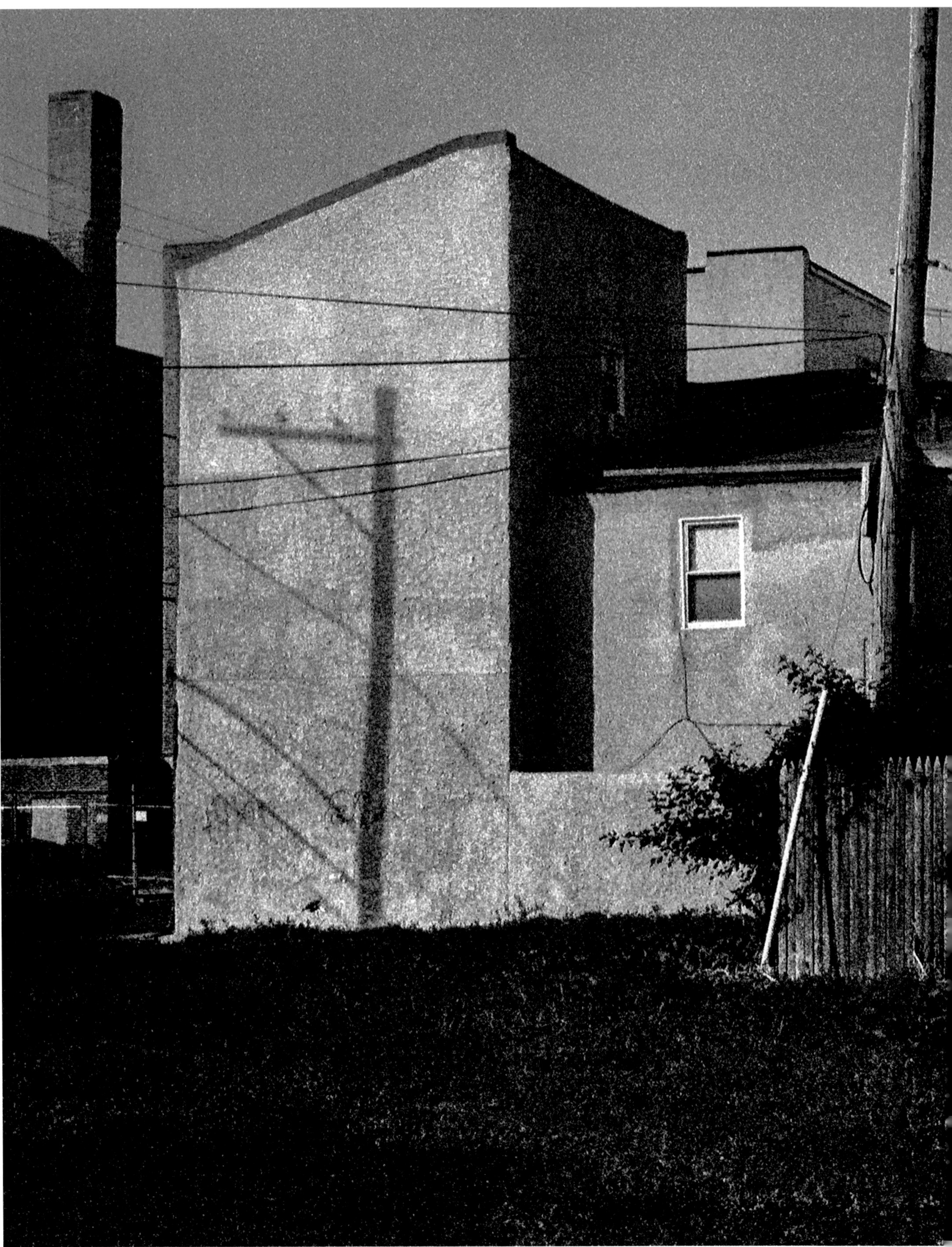

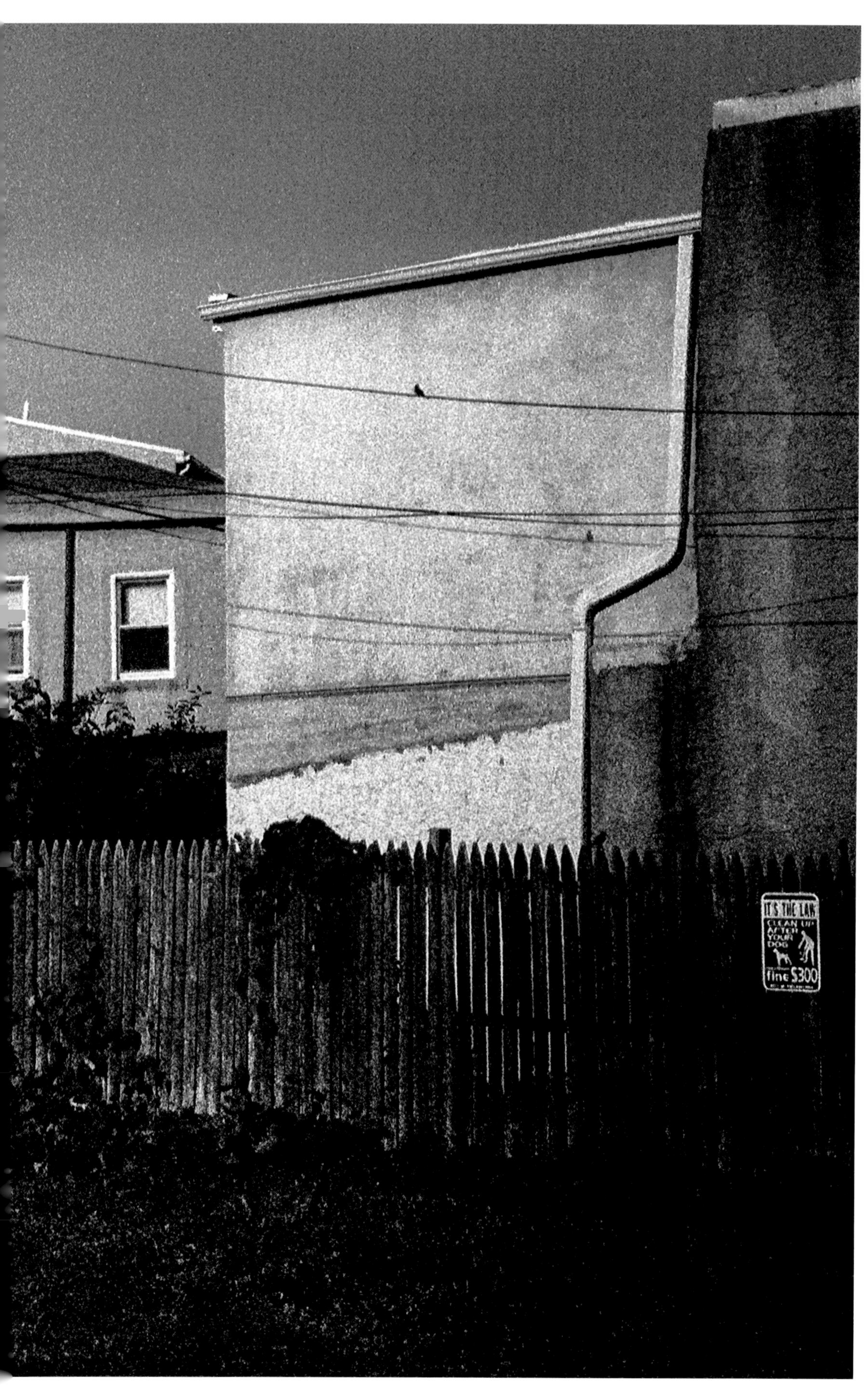

IT'S THE LAW
CLEAN UP
AFTER
YOUR
DOG
fine $300

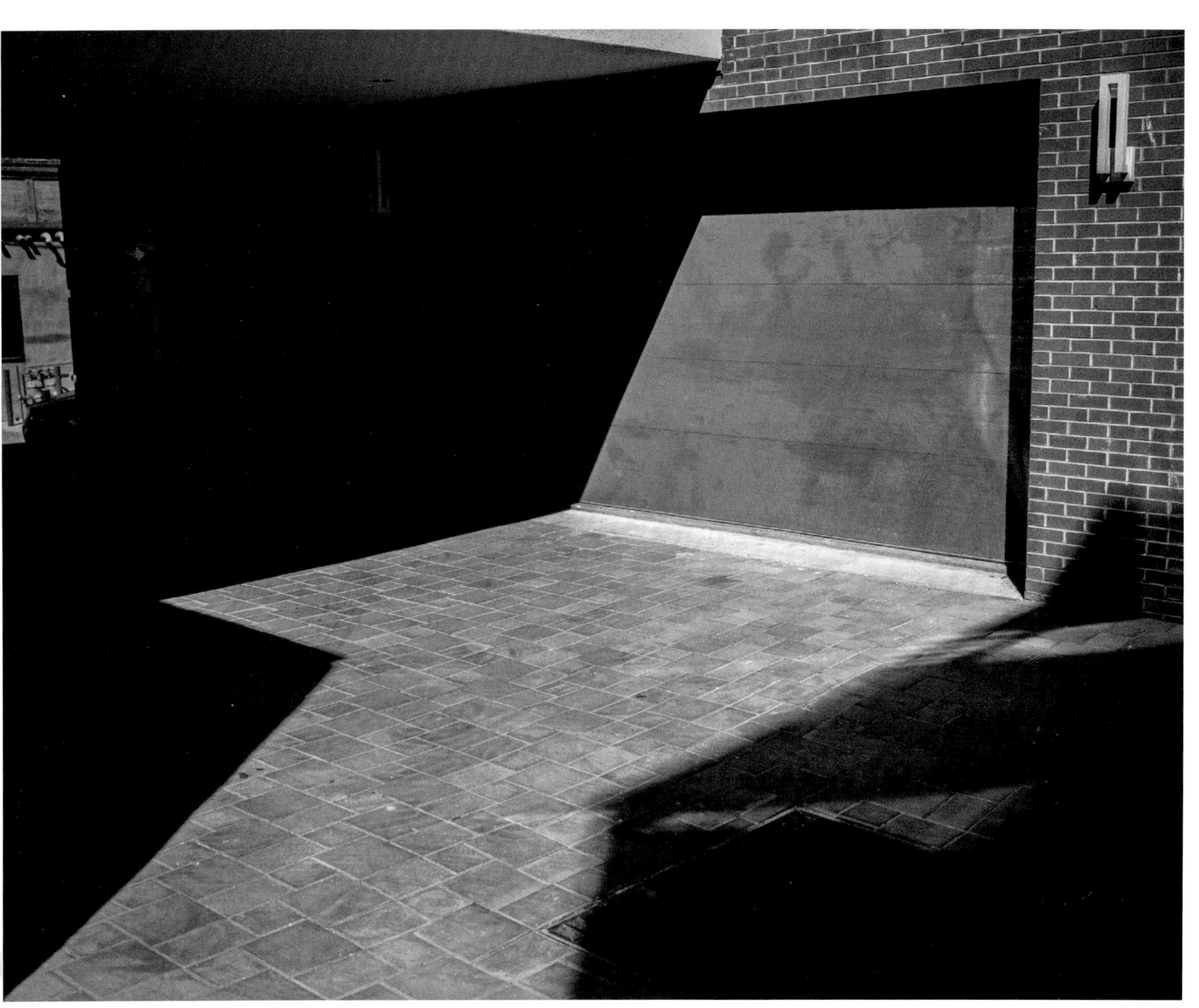

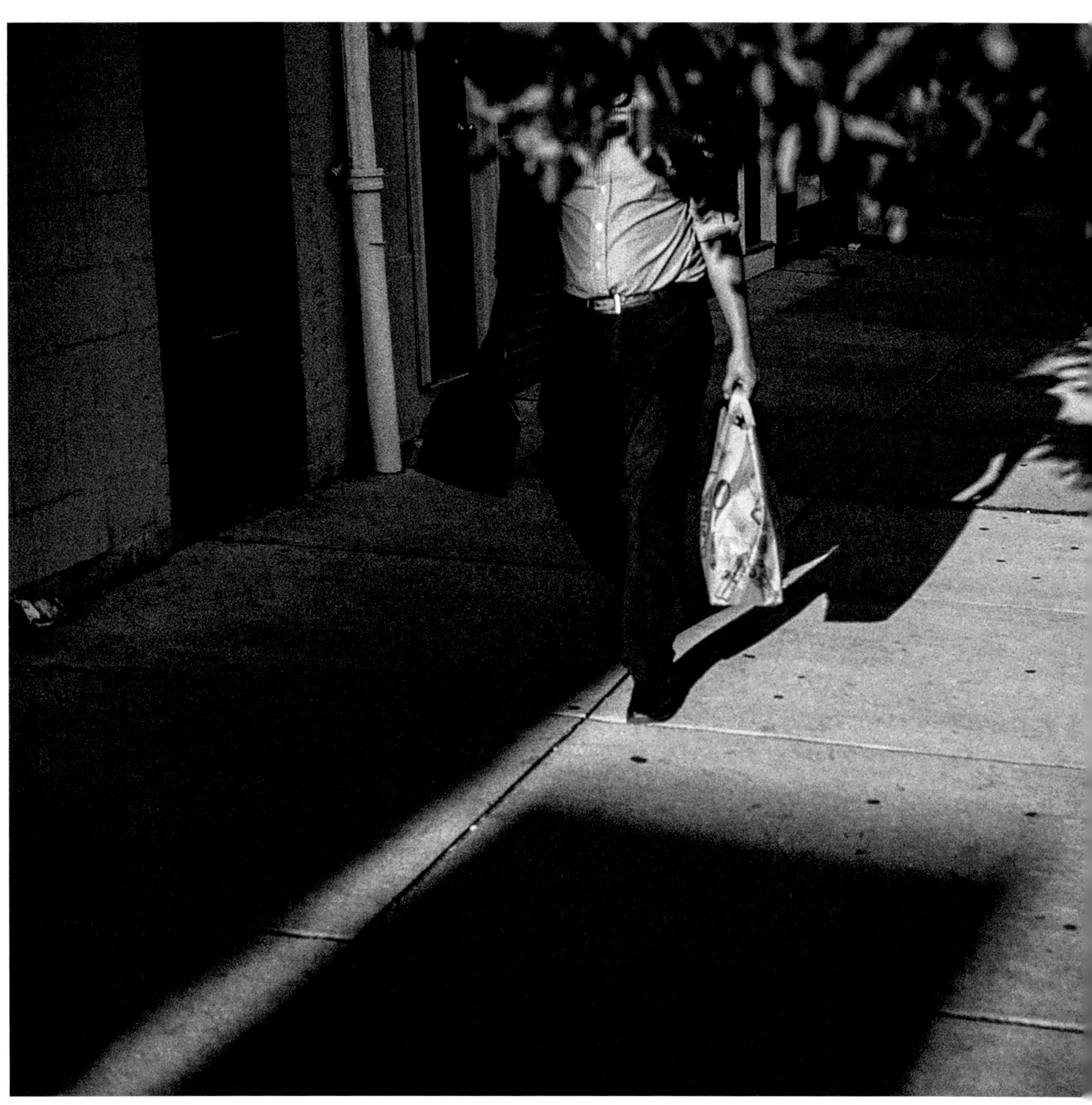

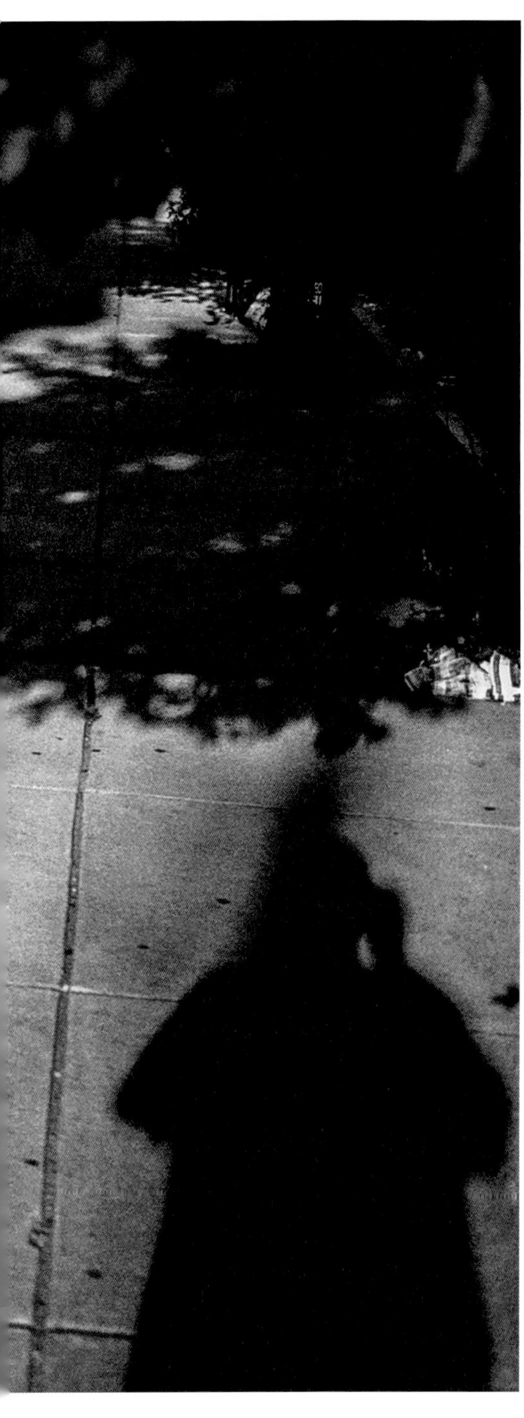

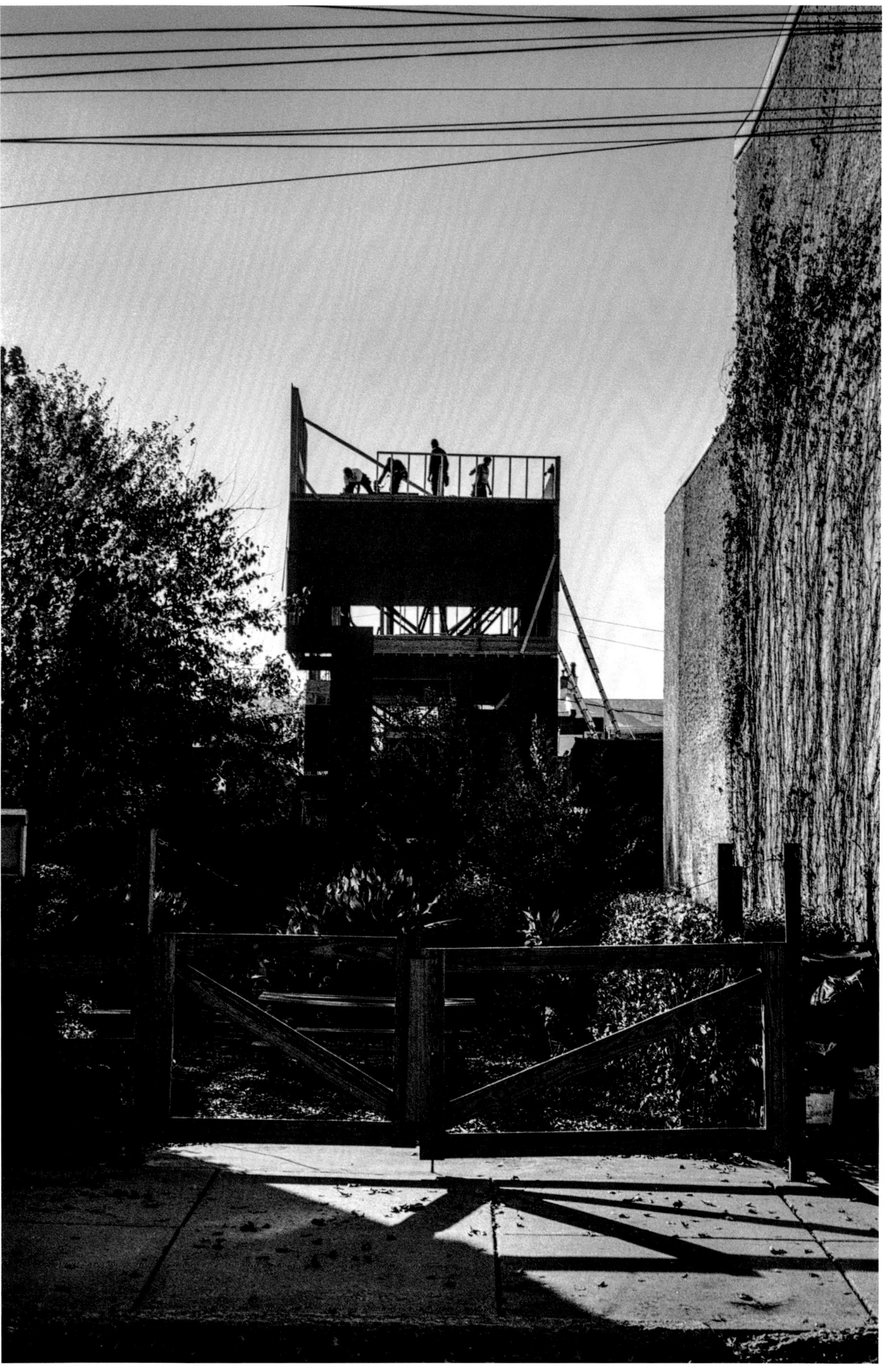

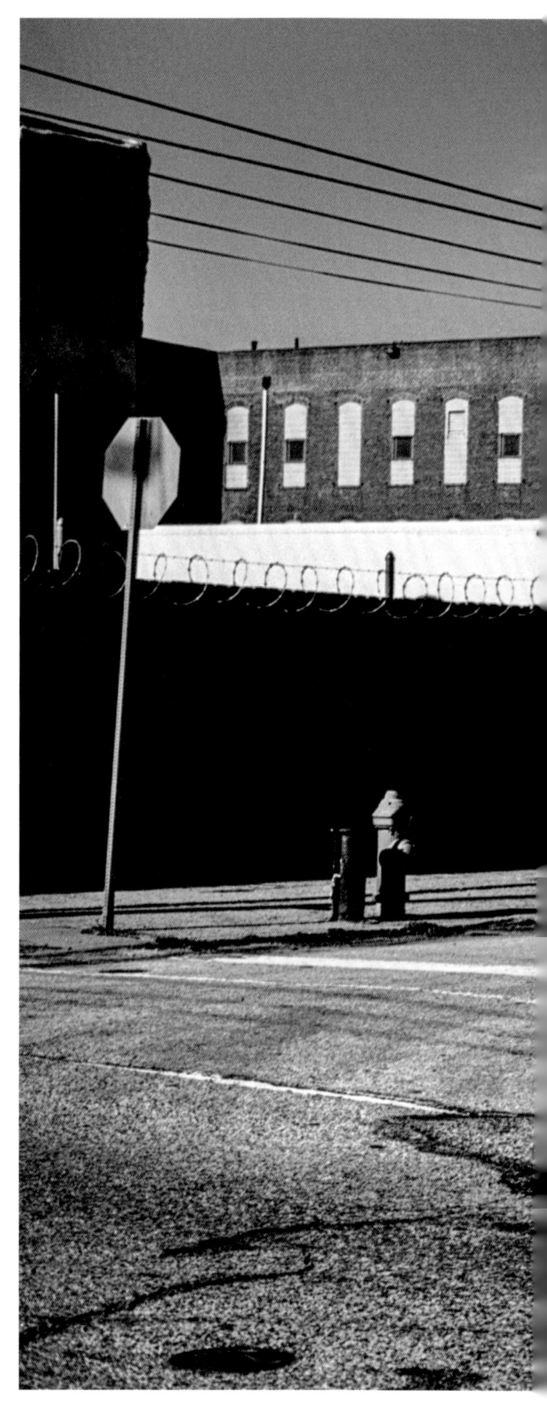

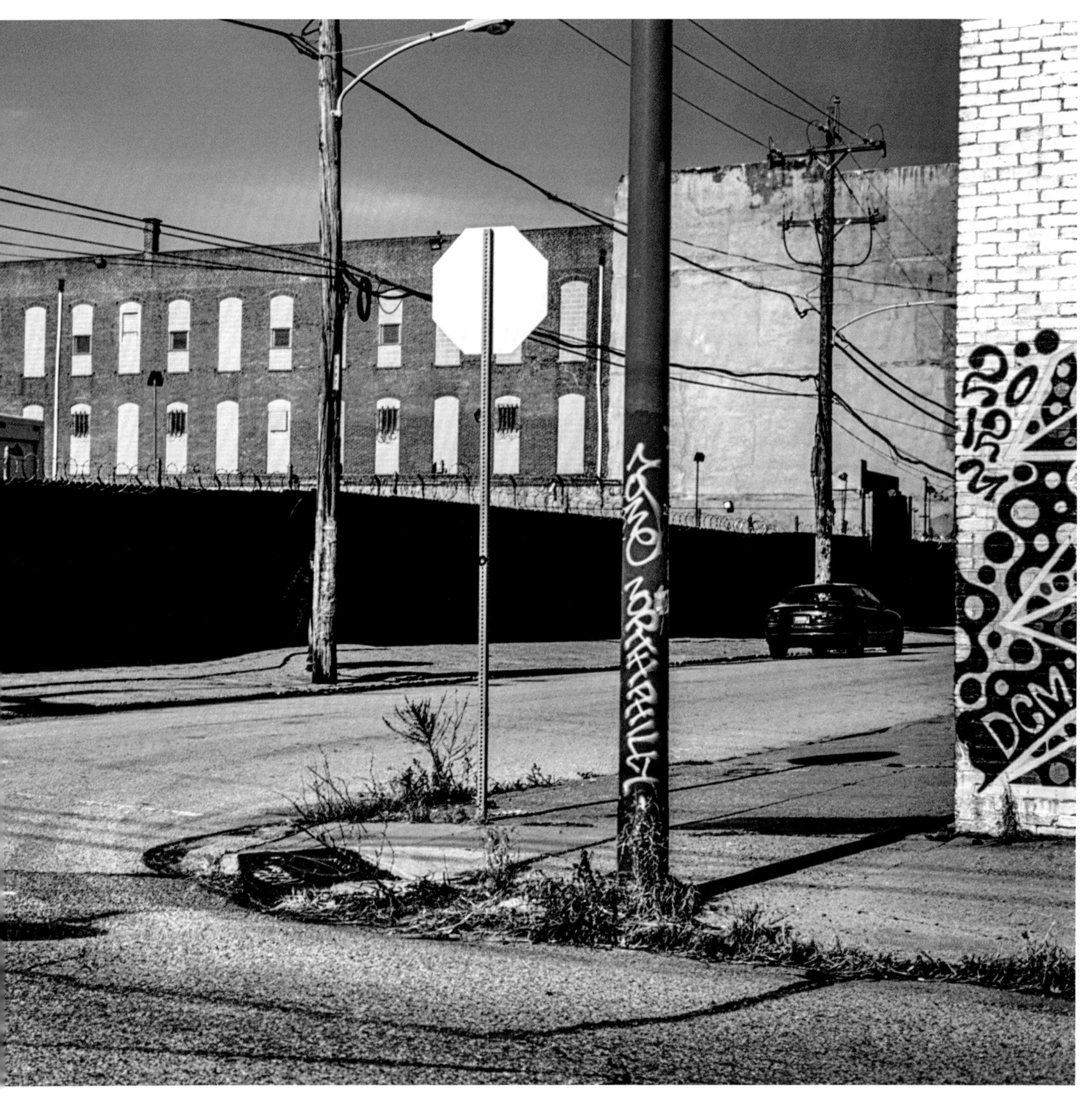

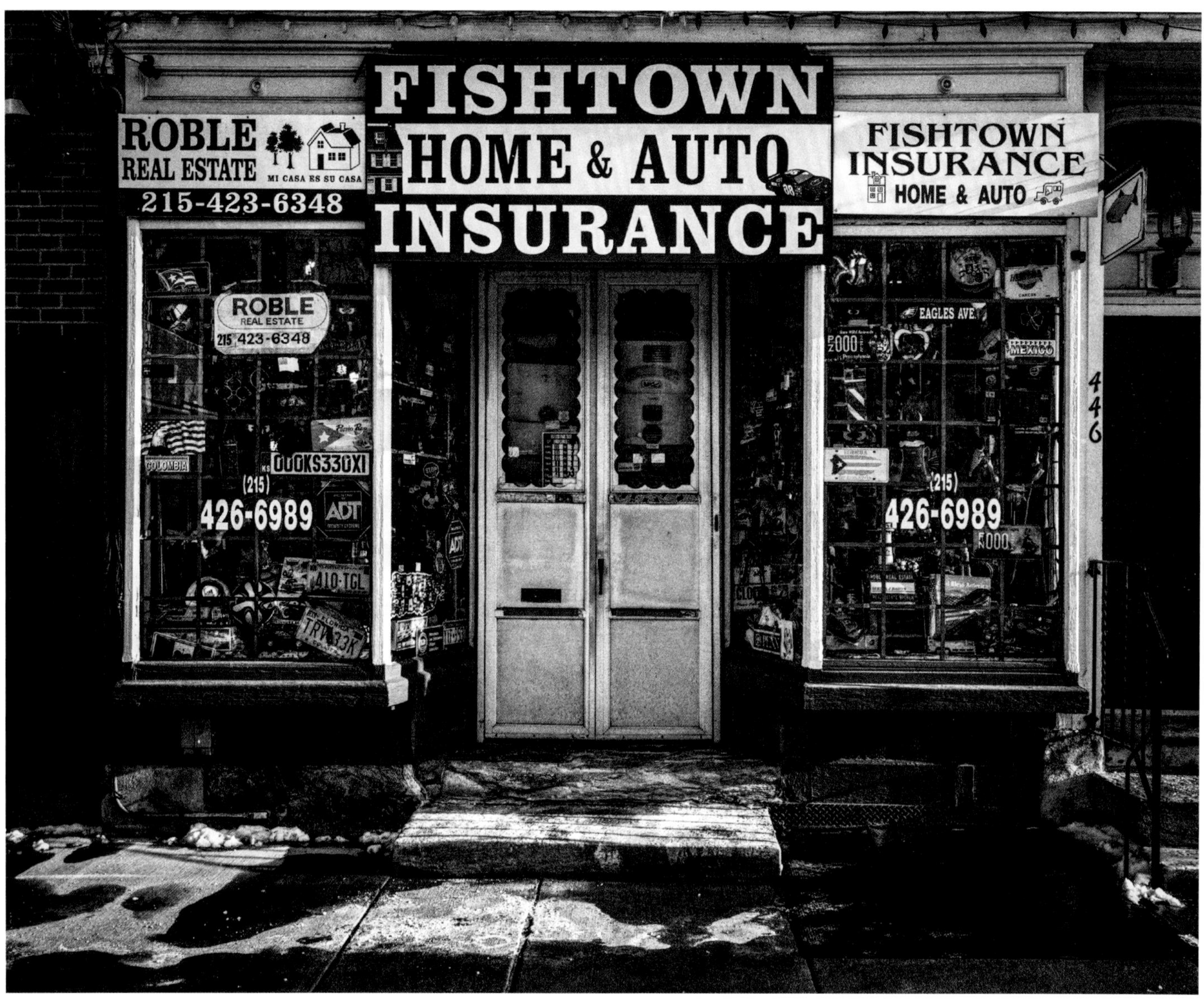
ROBLE REAL ESTATE
MI CASA ES SU CASA
215-423-6348
FISHTOWN HOME & AUTO INSURANCE
FISHTOWN INSURANCE
HOME & AUTO
ROBLE REAL ESTATE
215-423-6348
EAGLES AVE
MEXICO
COLOMBIA
(215) 426-6989
ADT
(215) 426-6989
446

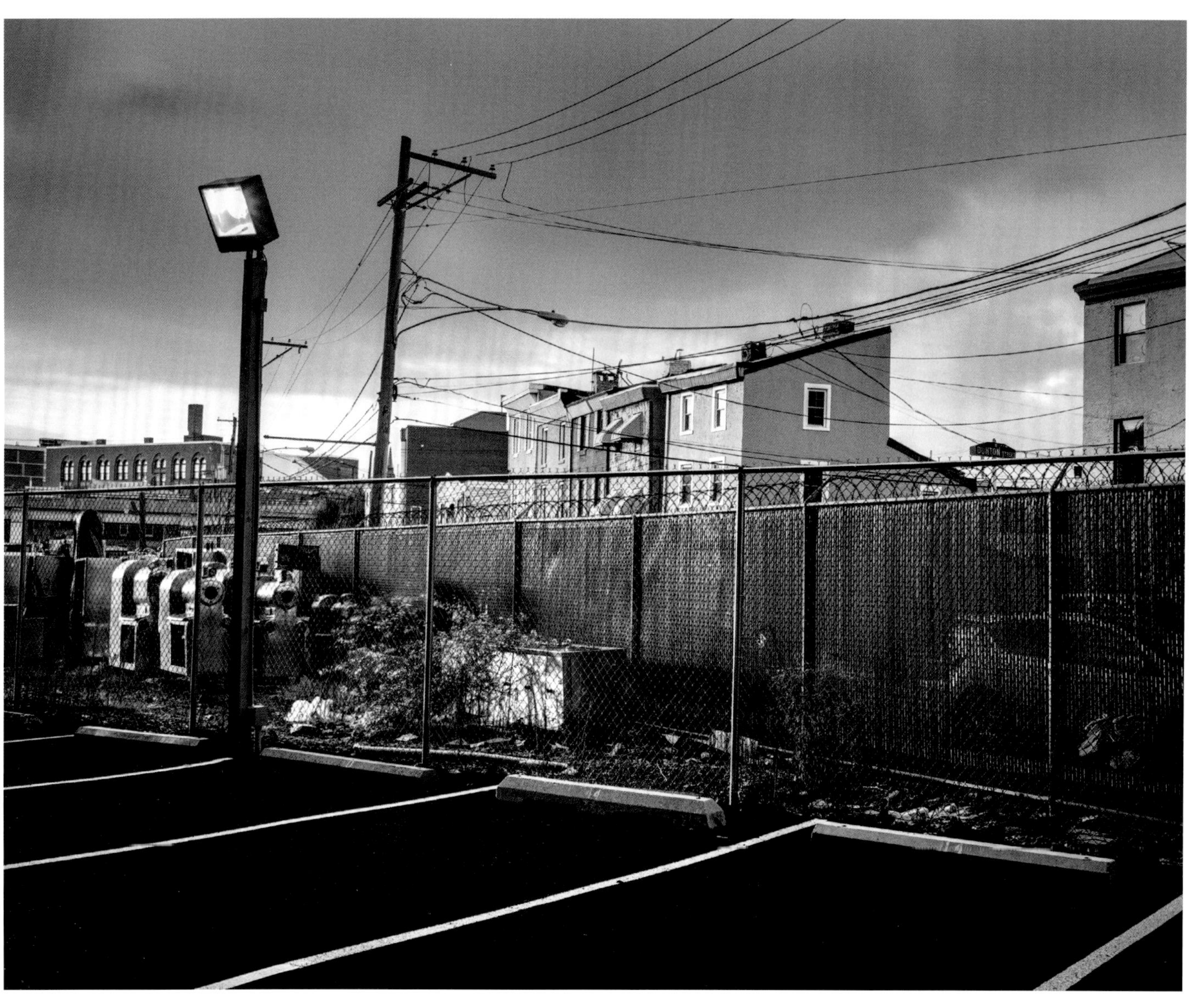

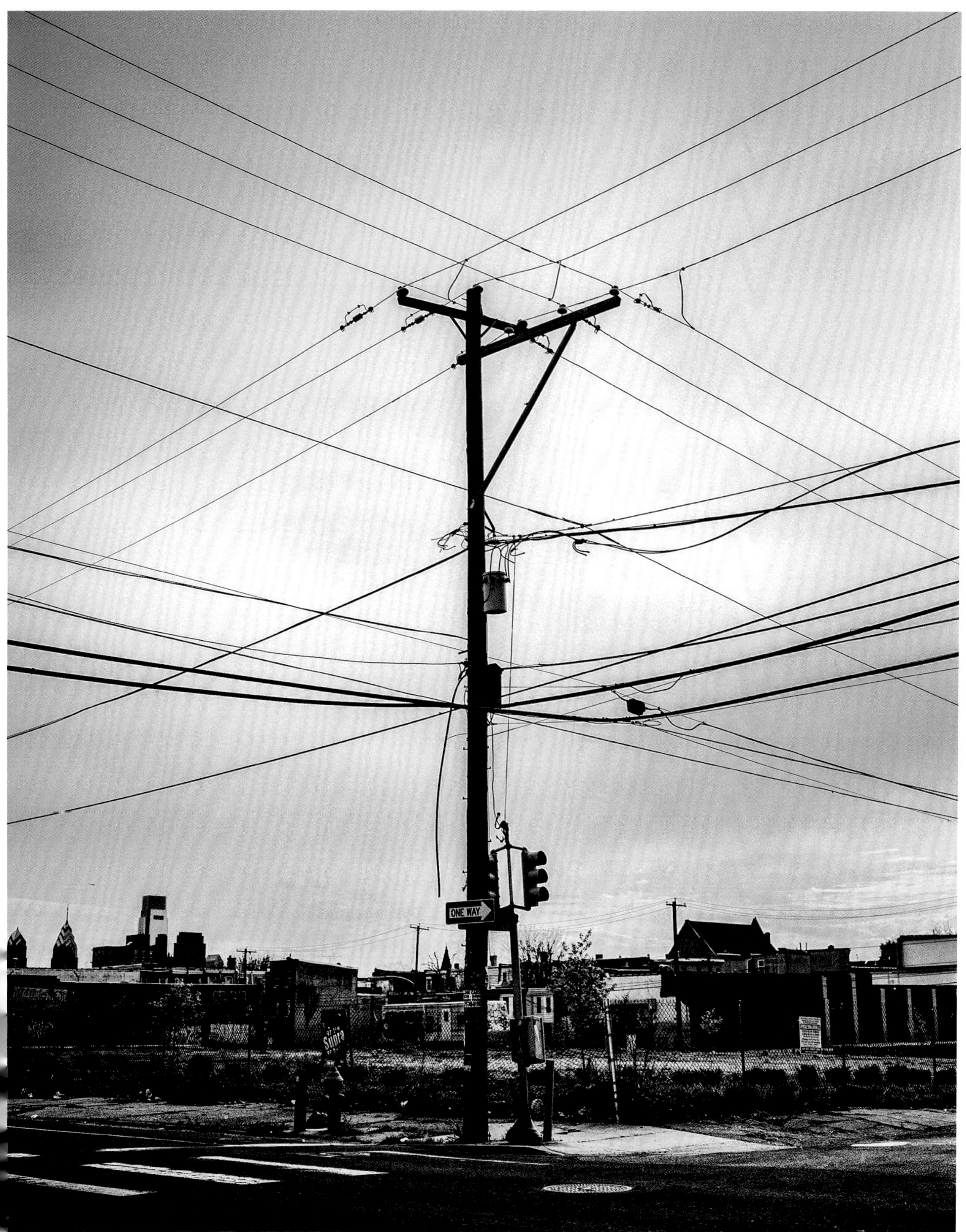

ONE WAY
Sugra

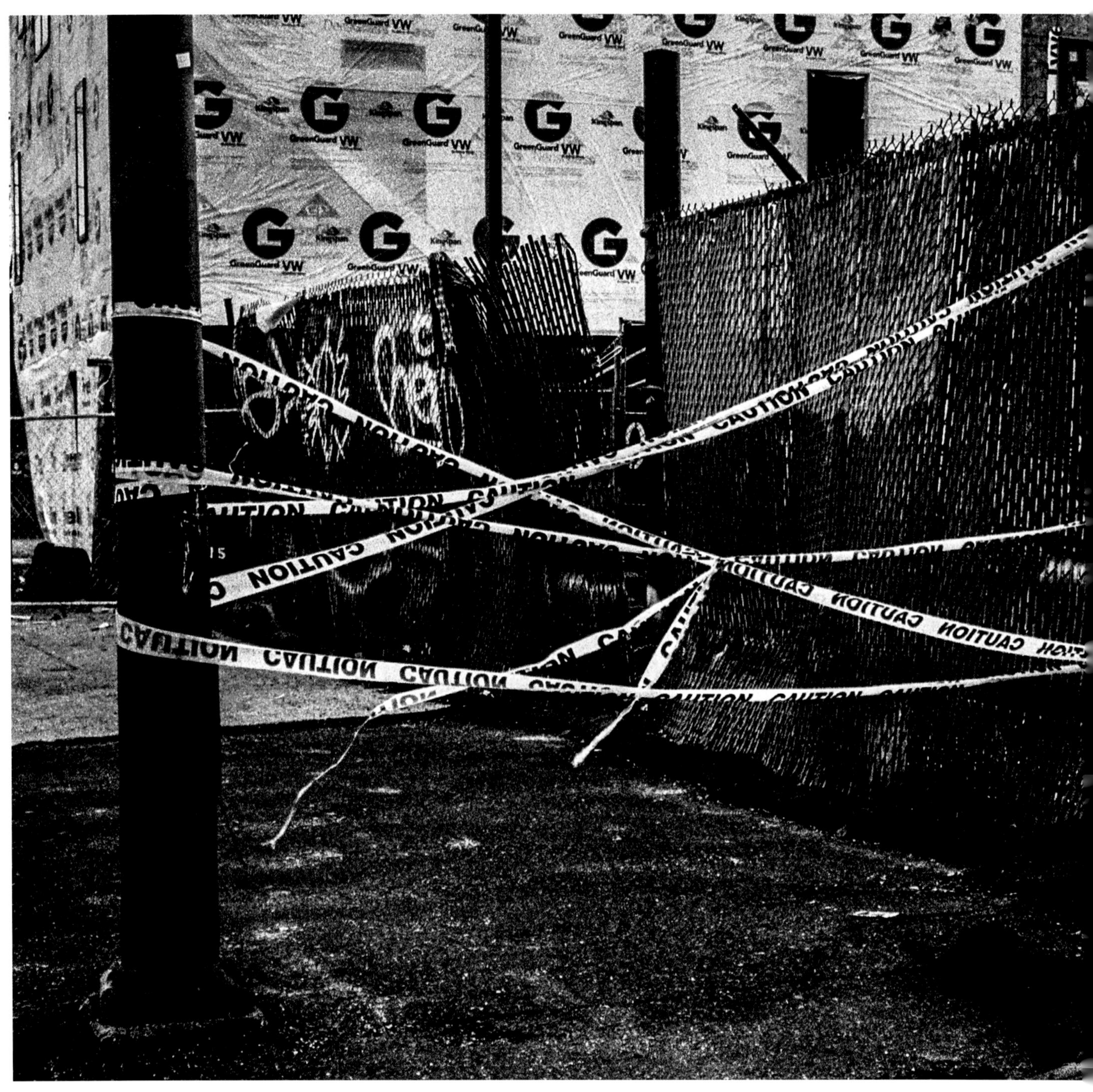

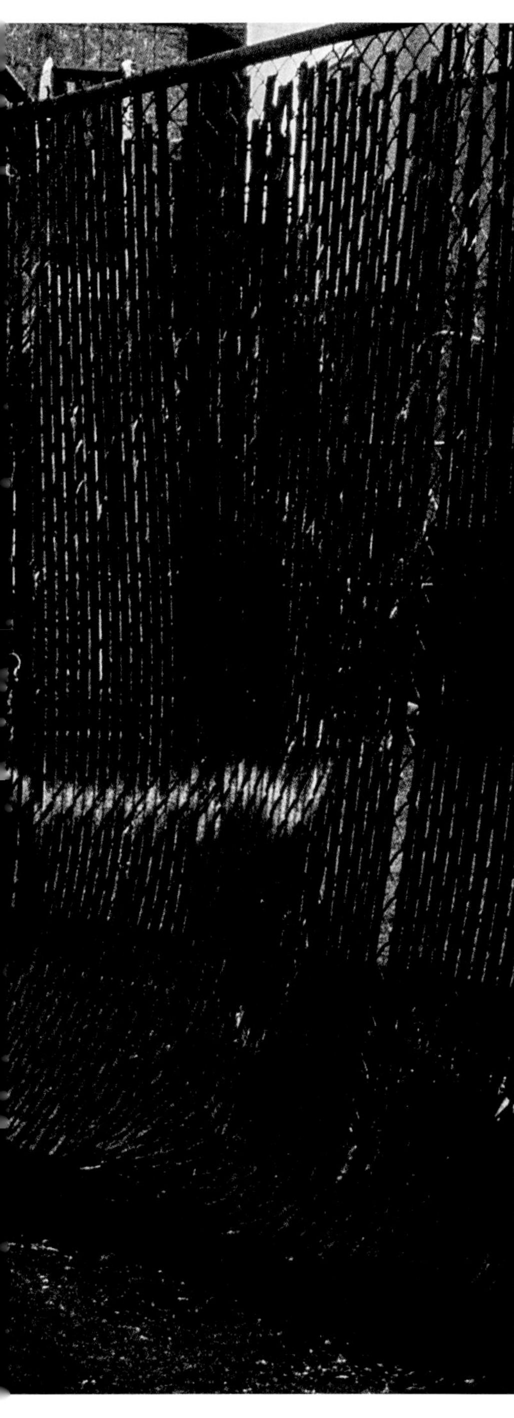

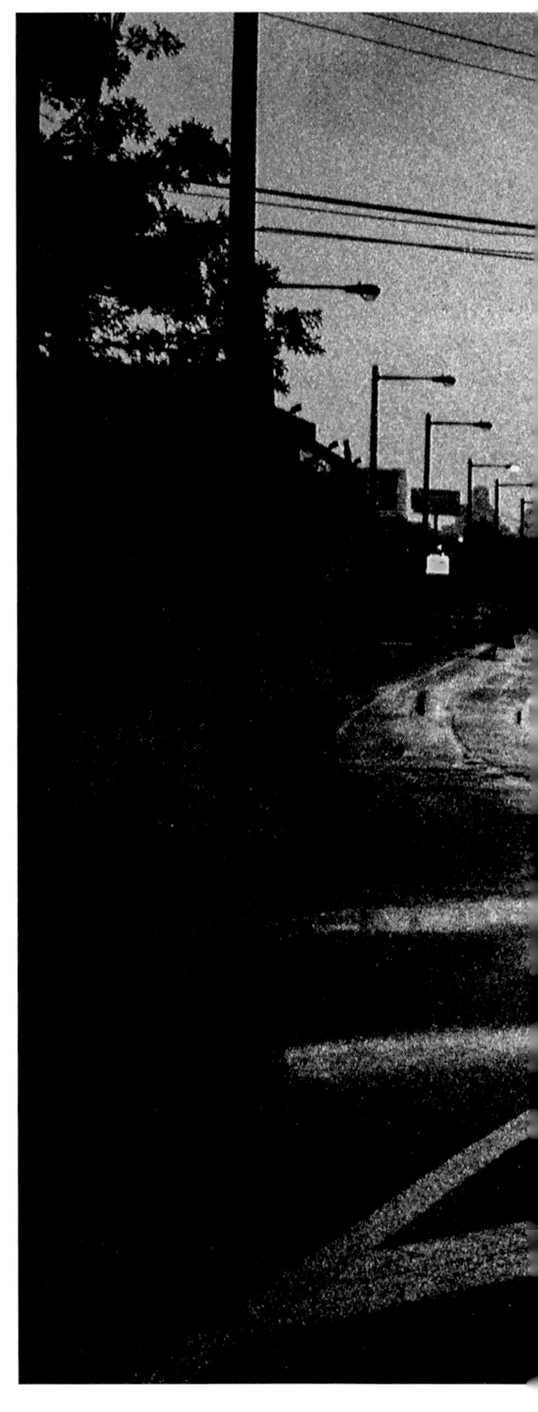

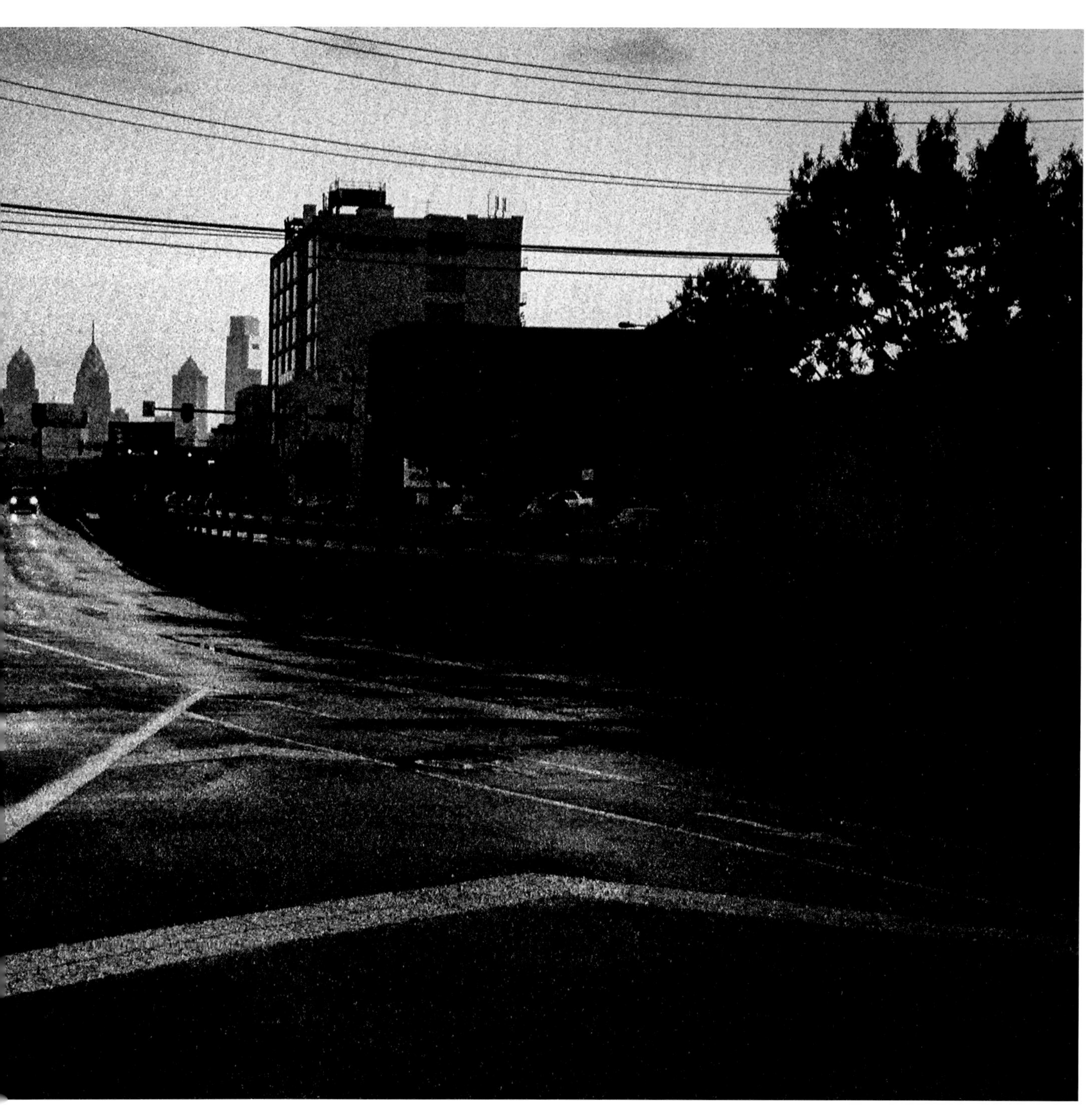

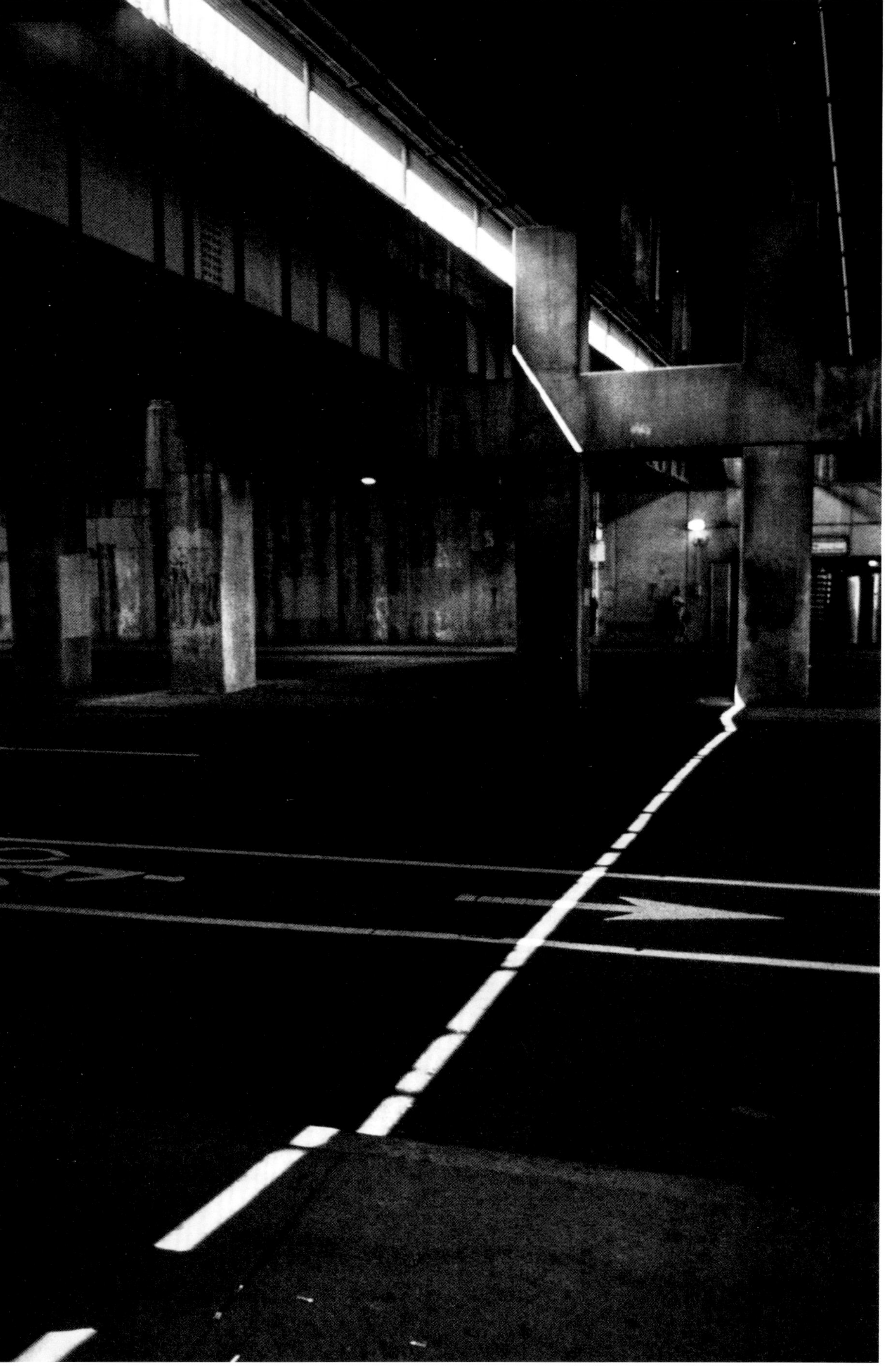

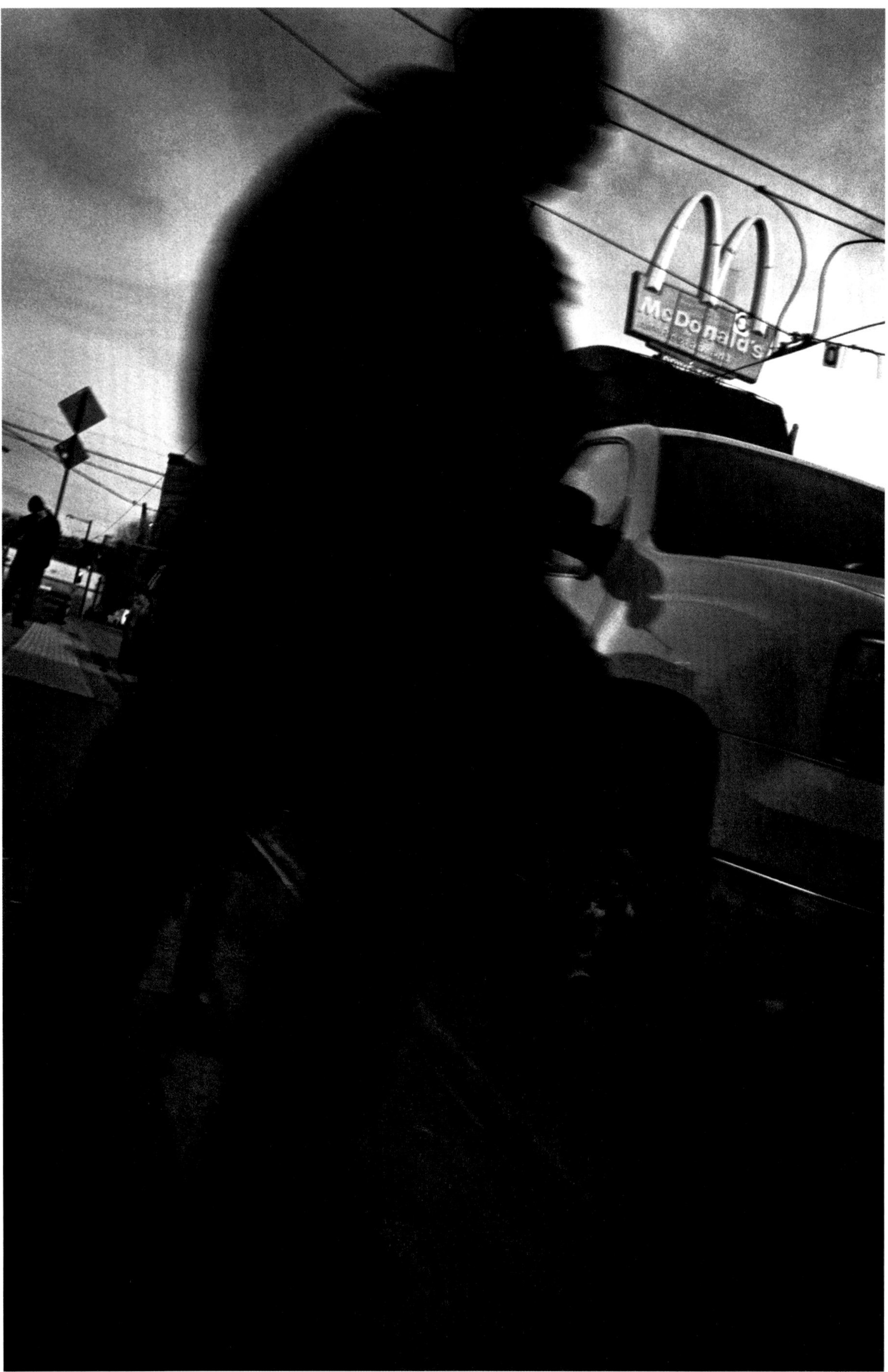

McDonald's

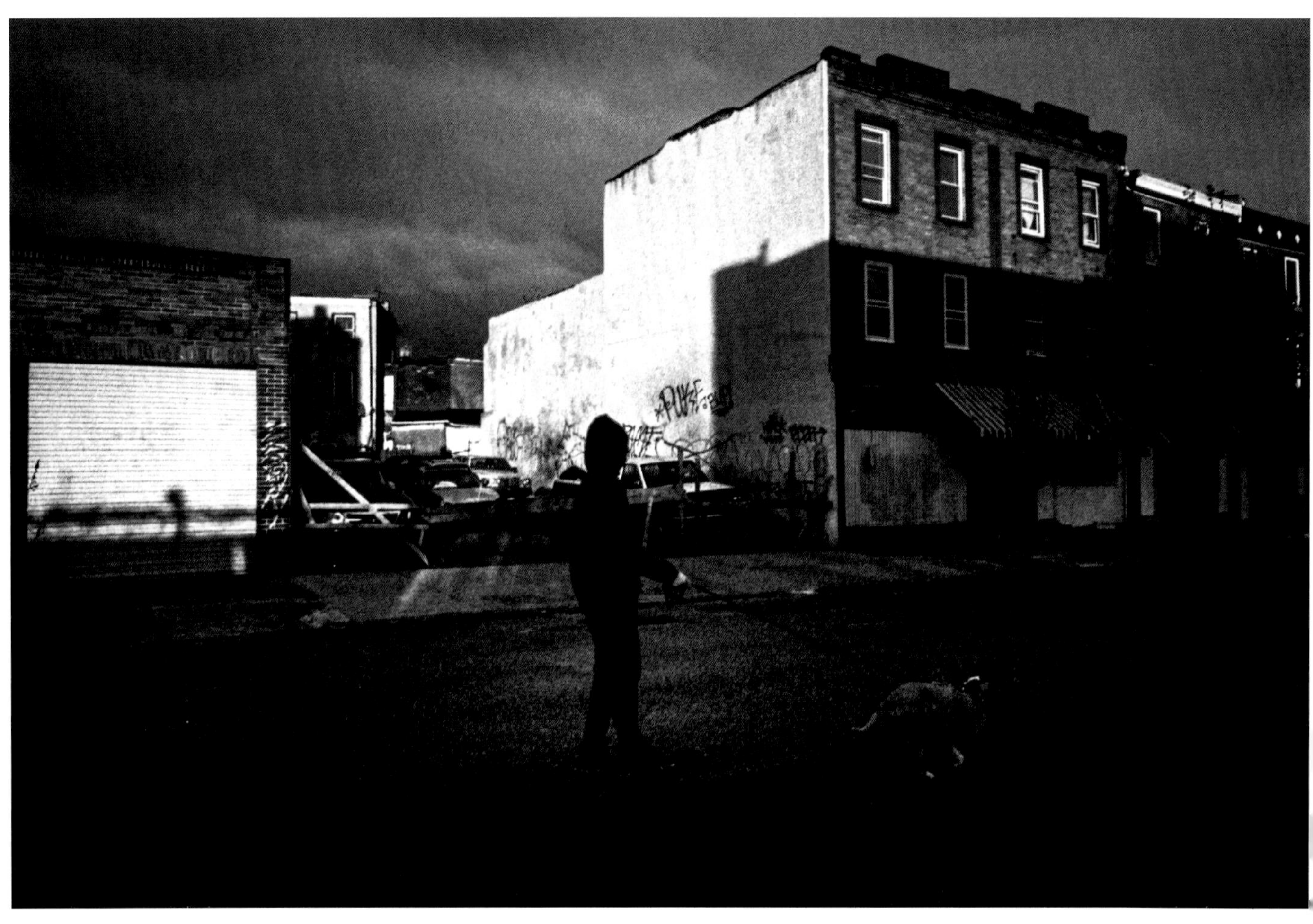

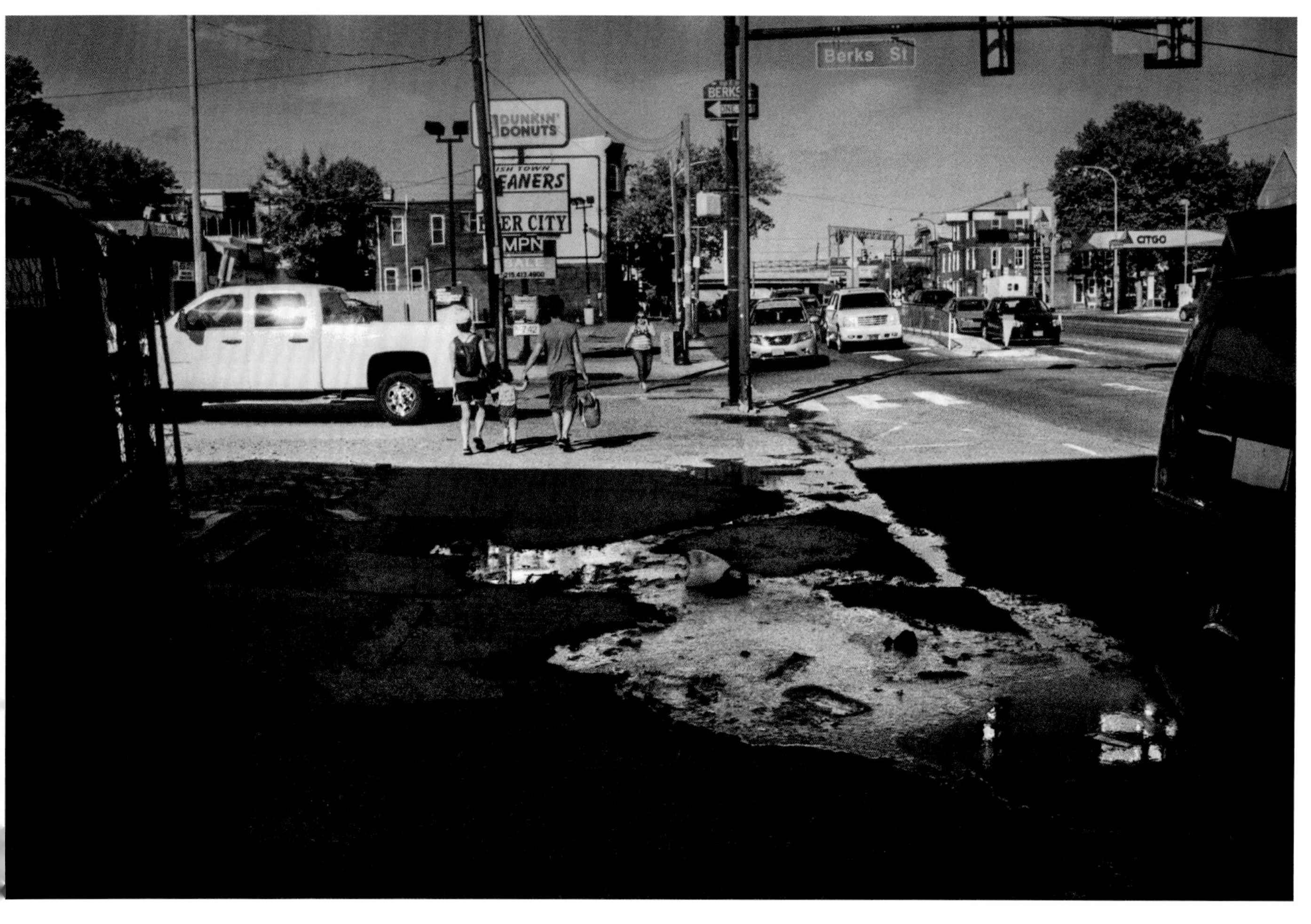
Berks St
BERKS
DUNKIN' DONUTS
ISH TOWN
CLEANERS
ER CITY
MPN
CITGO

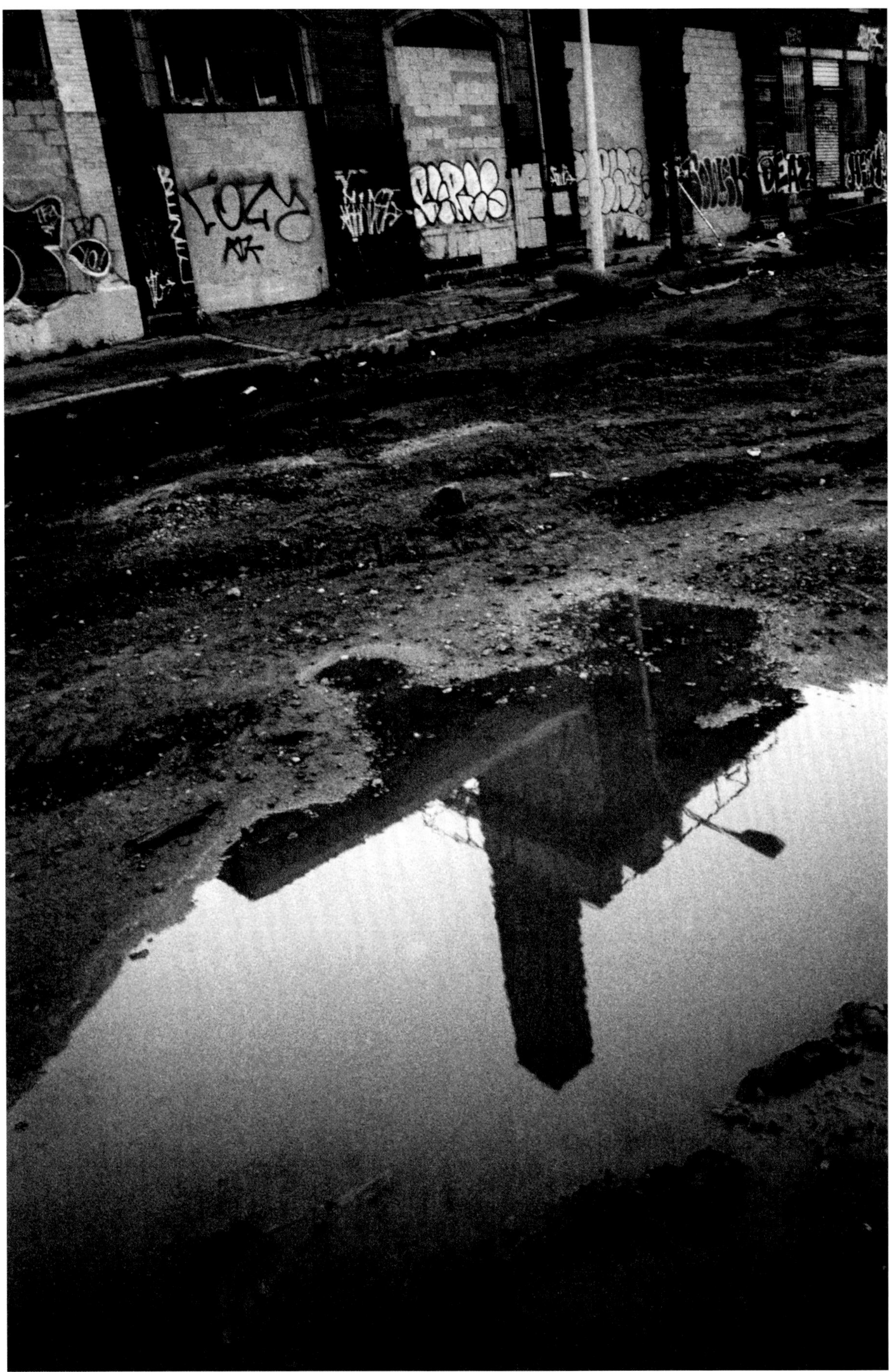

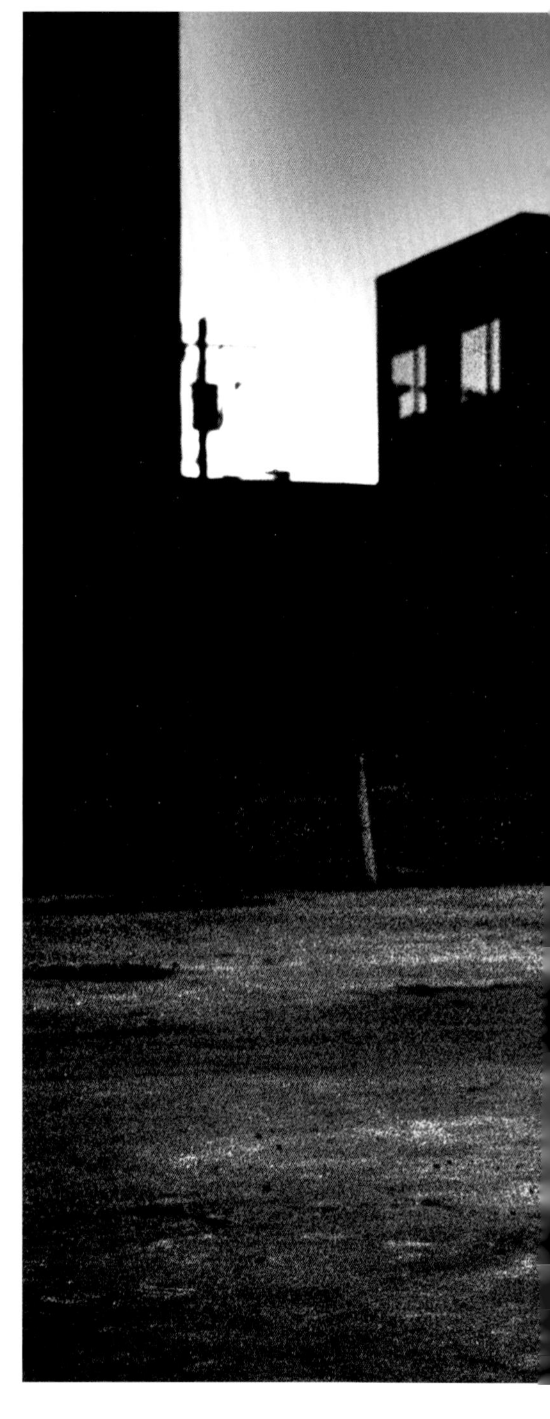

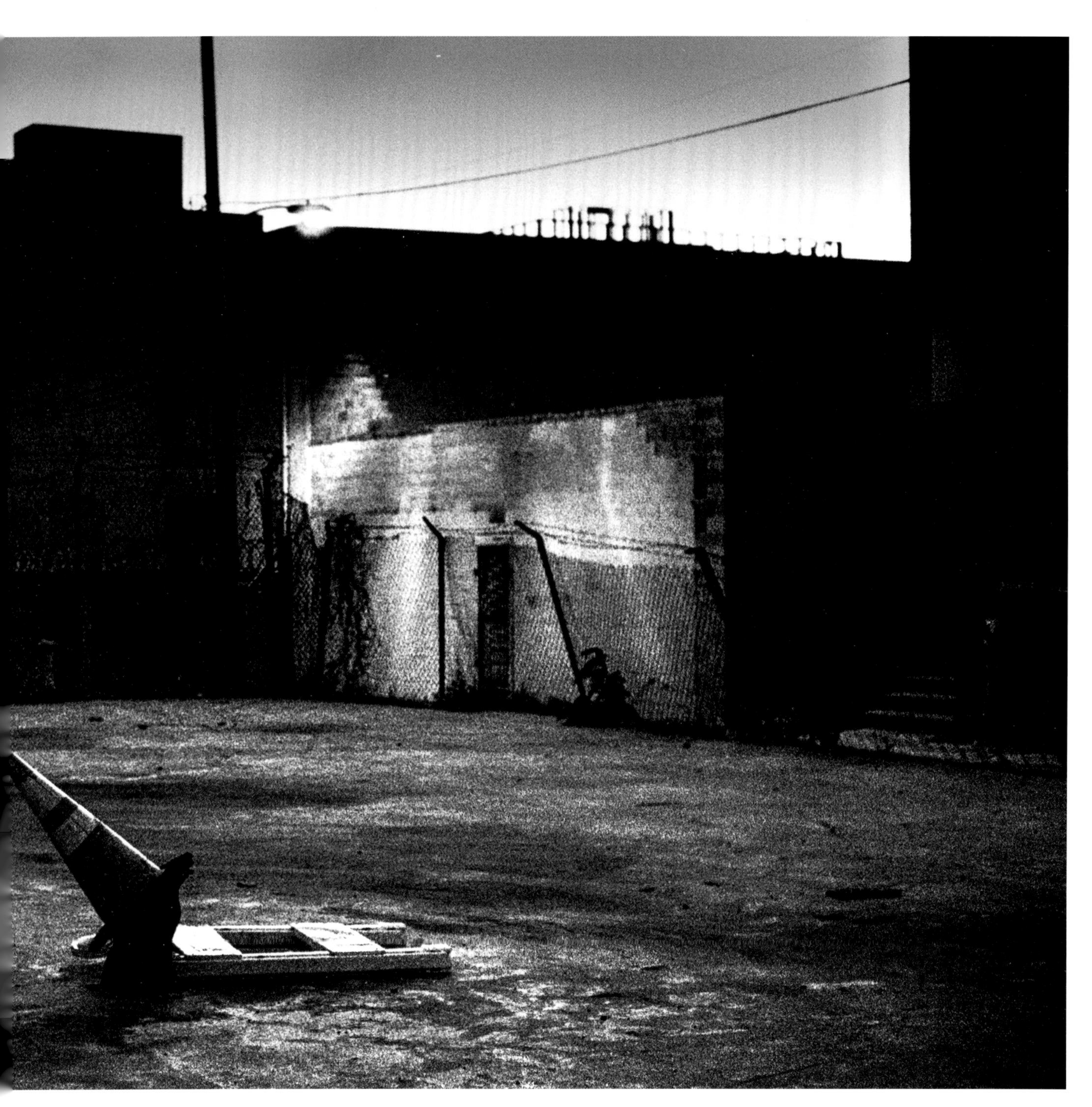

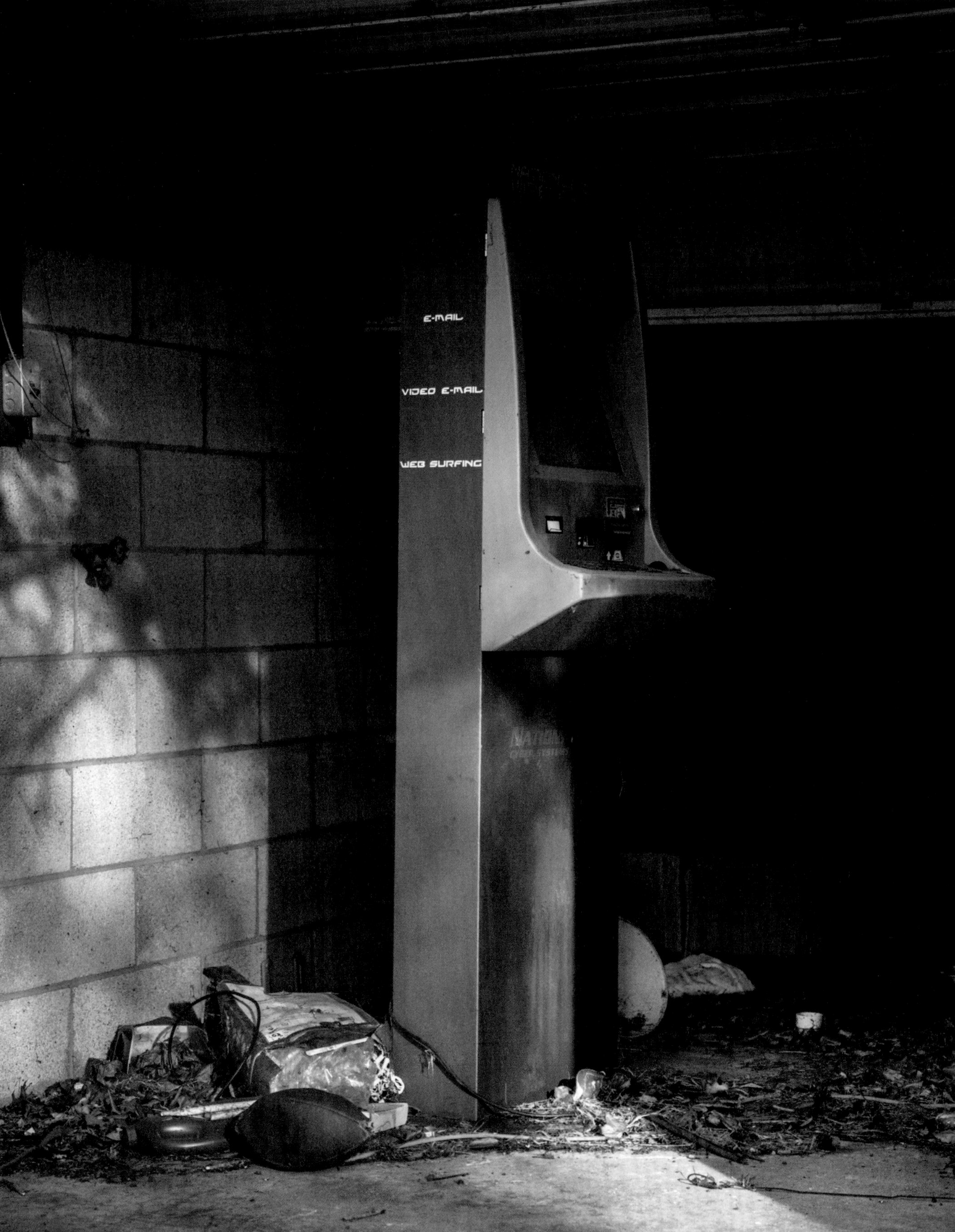

E-MAIL
VIDEO E-MAIL
WEB SURFING

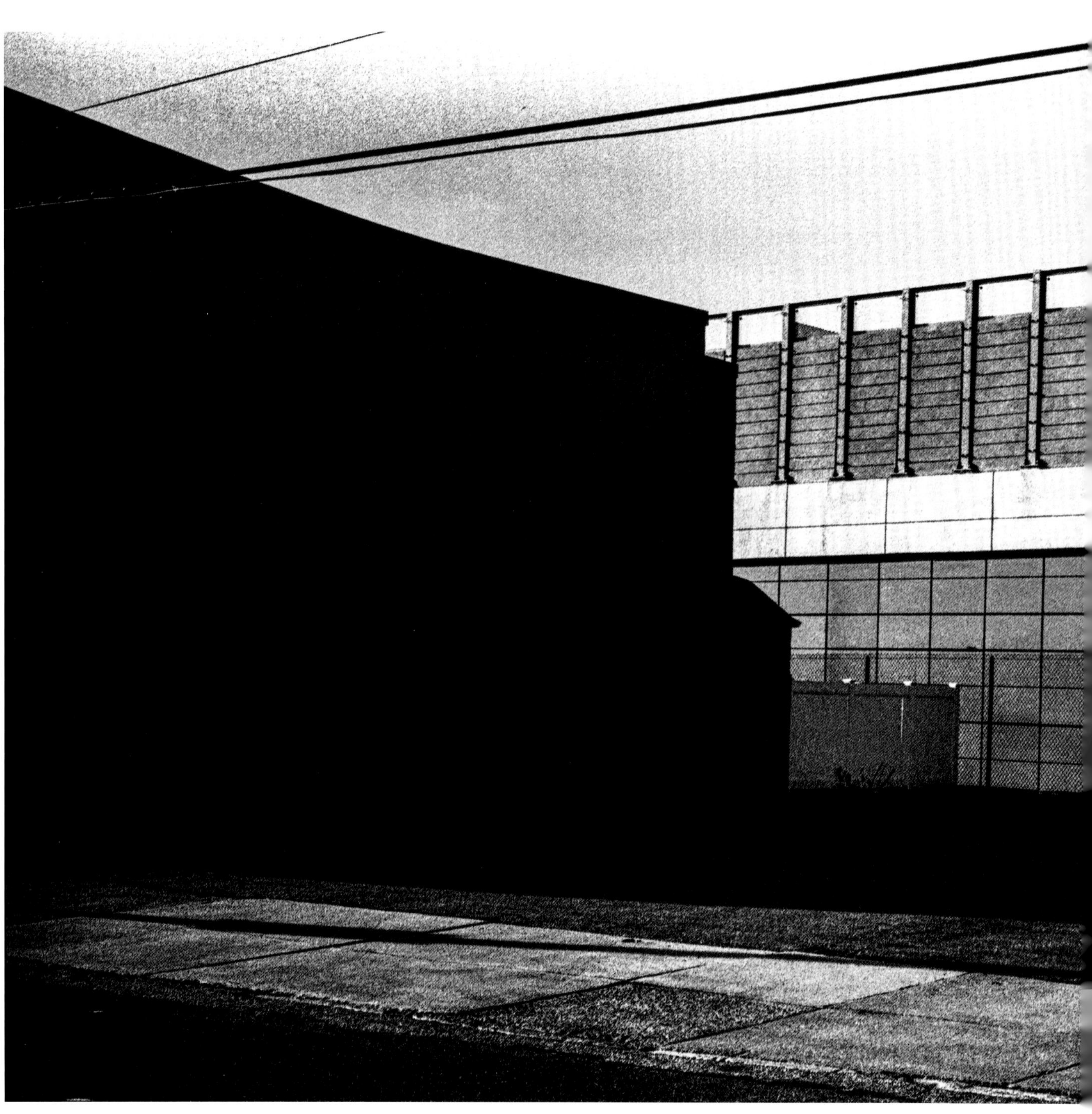

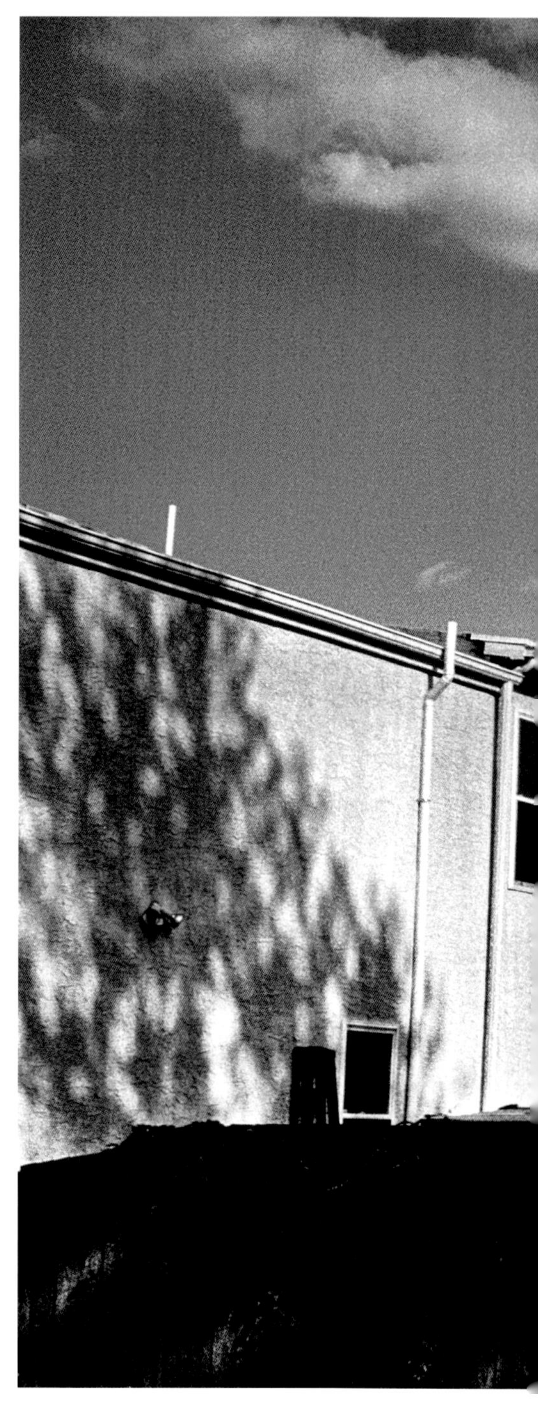

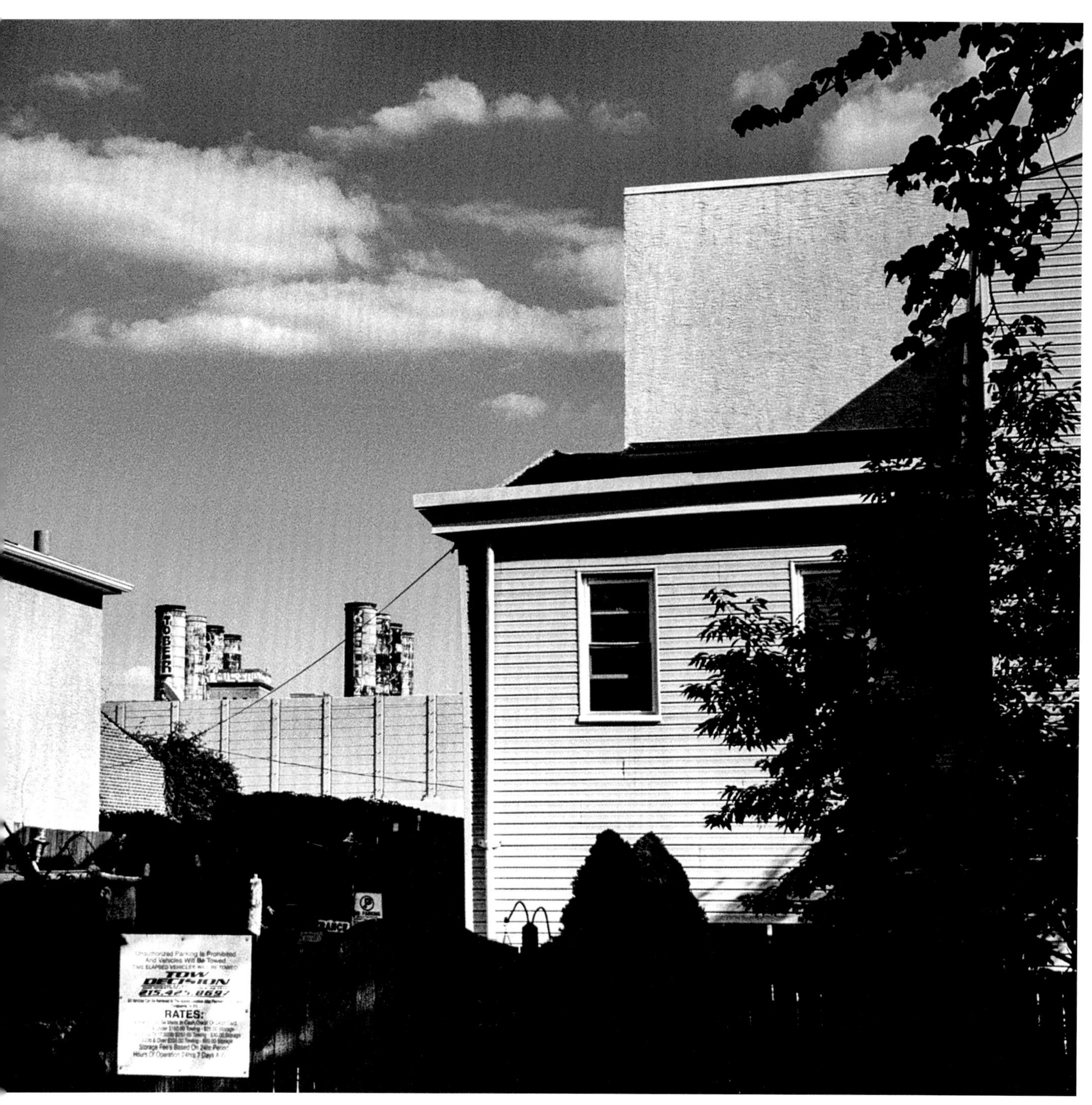
Unauthorized Parking Is Prohibited
And Vehicles Will Be Towed!
TIME ELAPSED VEHICLES WILL BE TOWED
TOW
DECISION
215.423.8697
RATES:
Storage Fees Based On 24hr Period
Hours Of Operation 24hrs 7 Days A Week

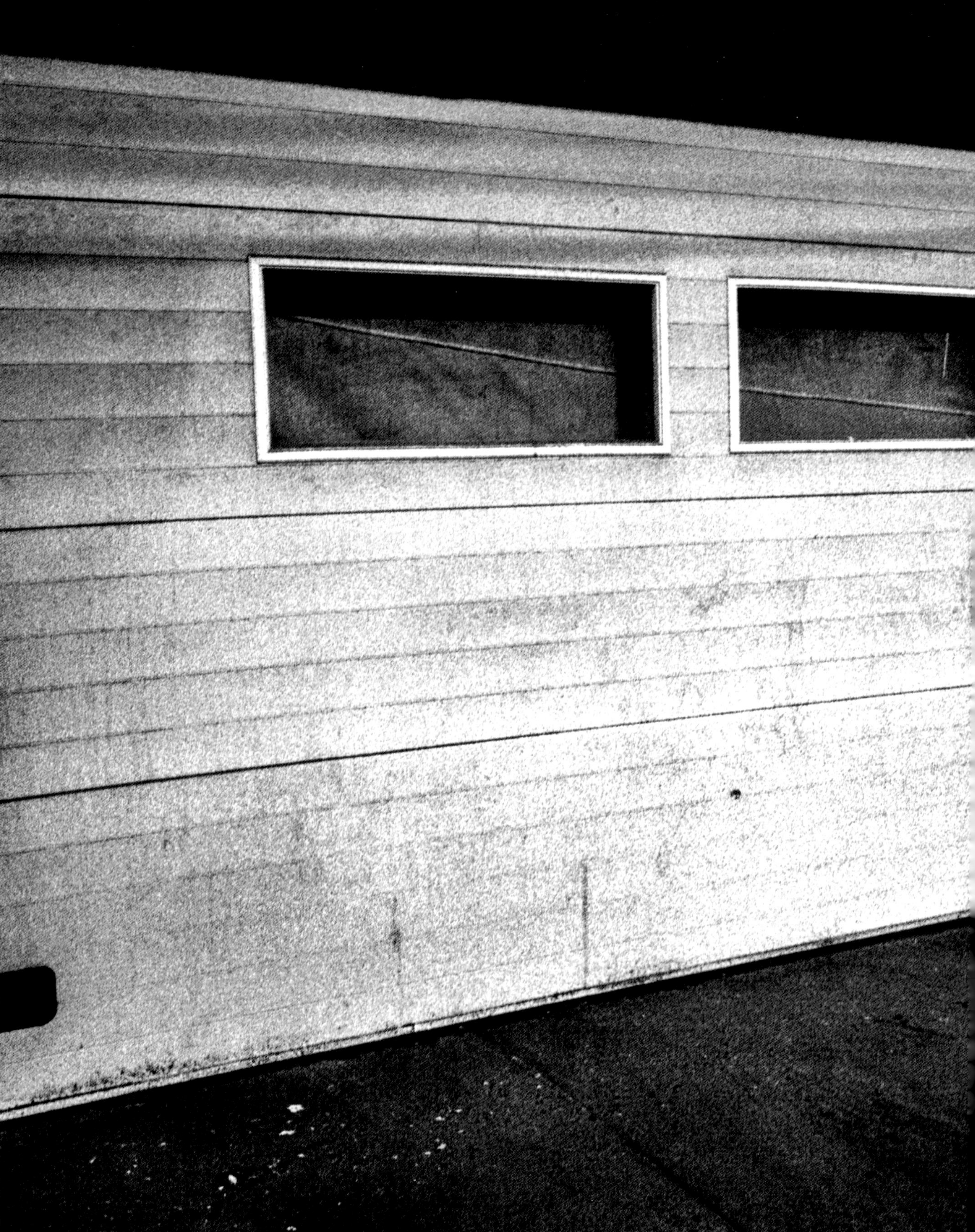

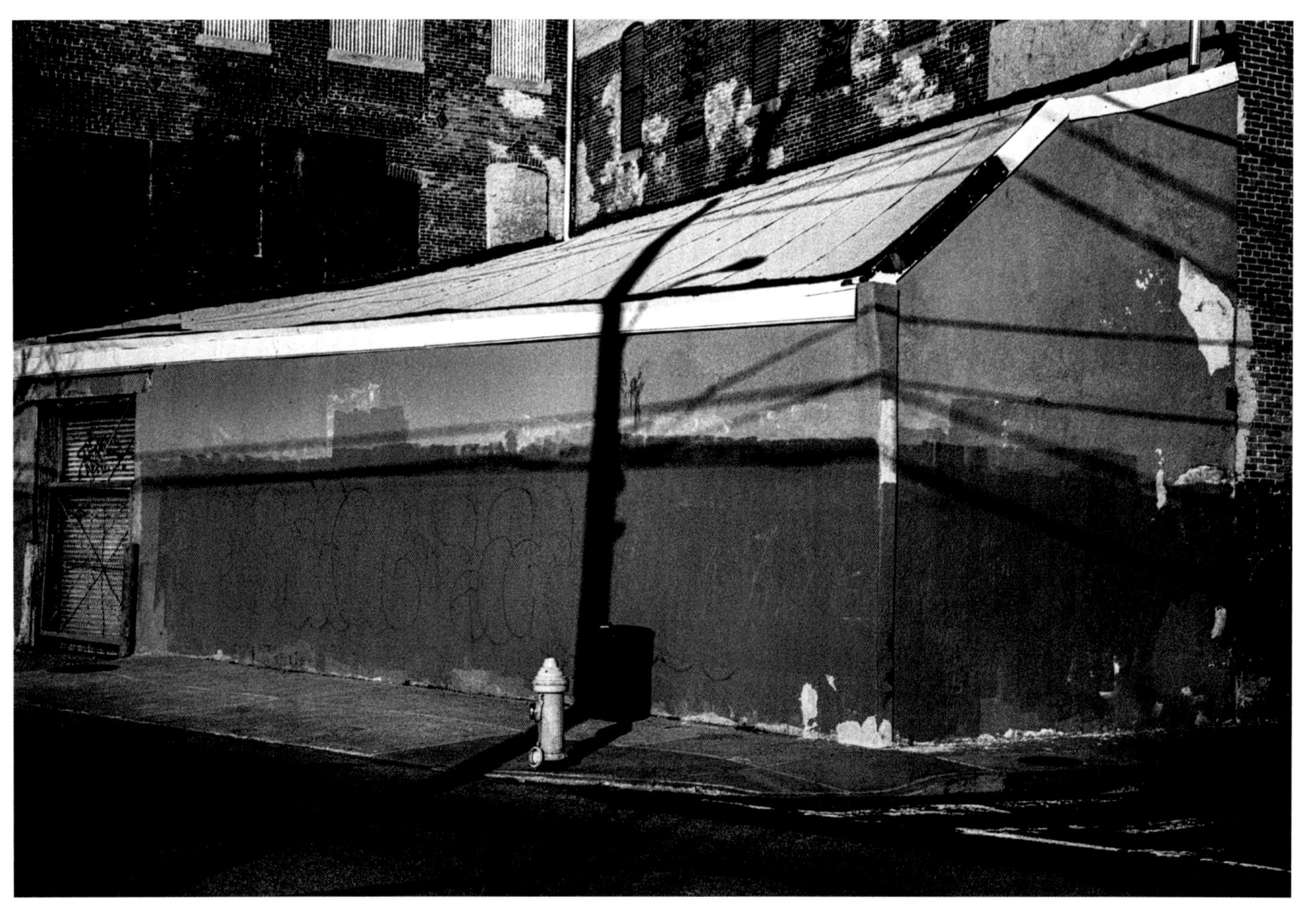

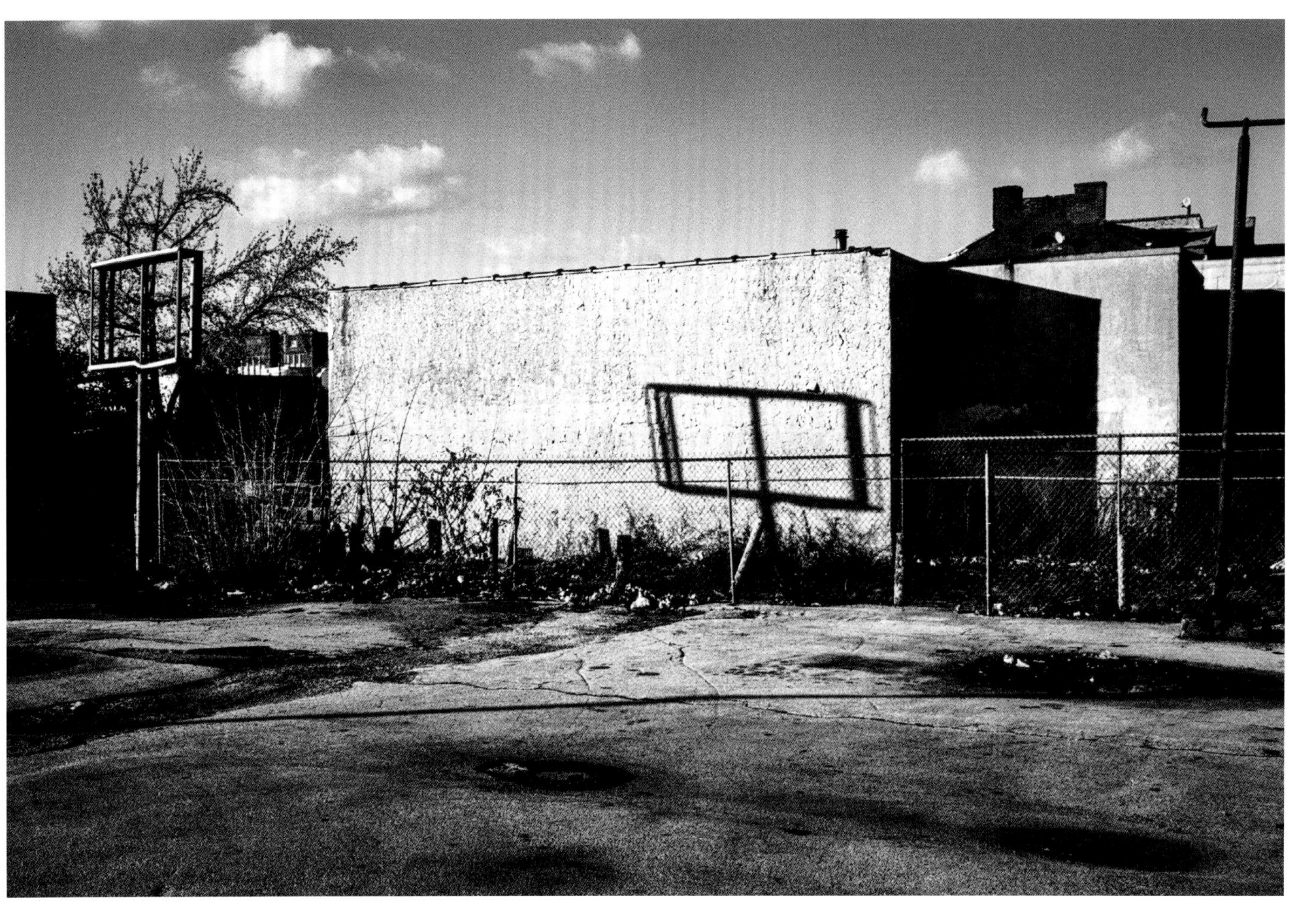

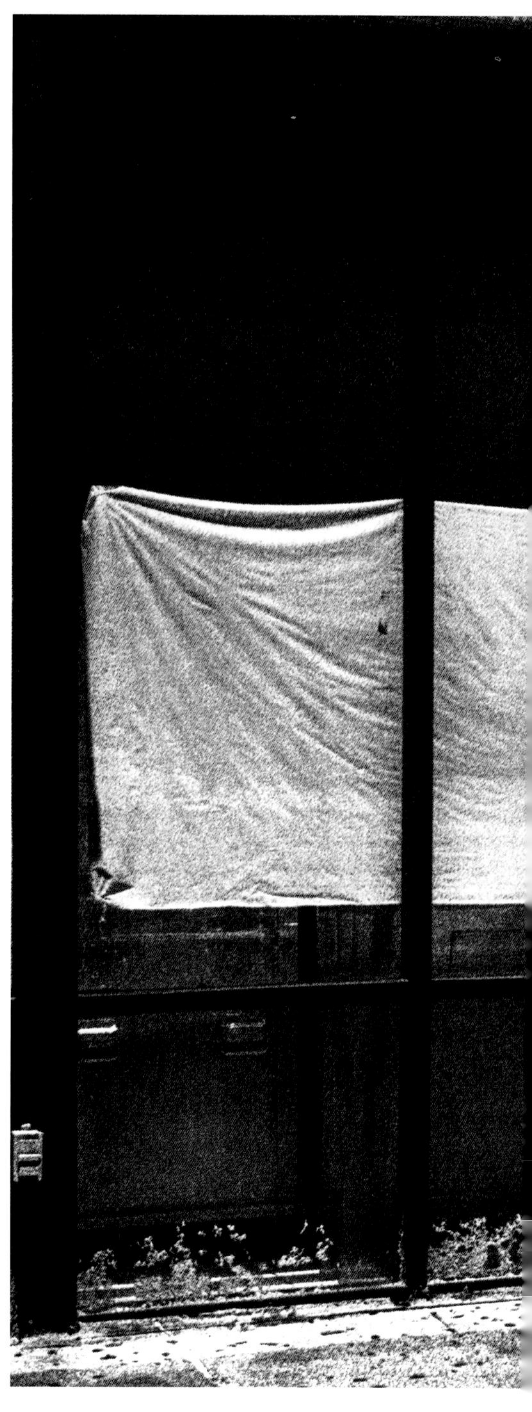

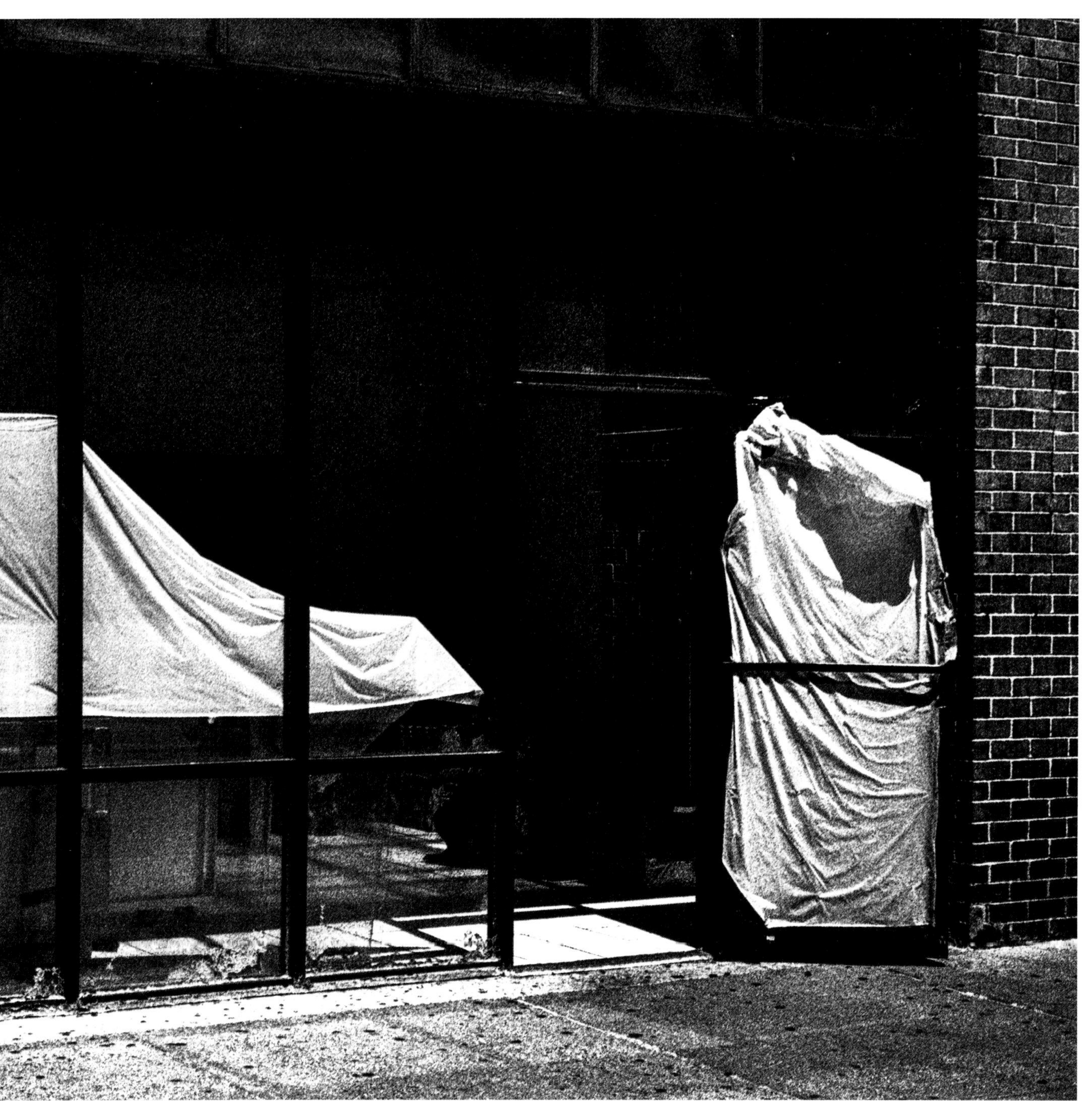

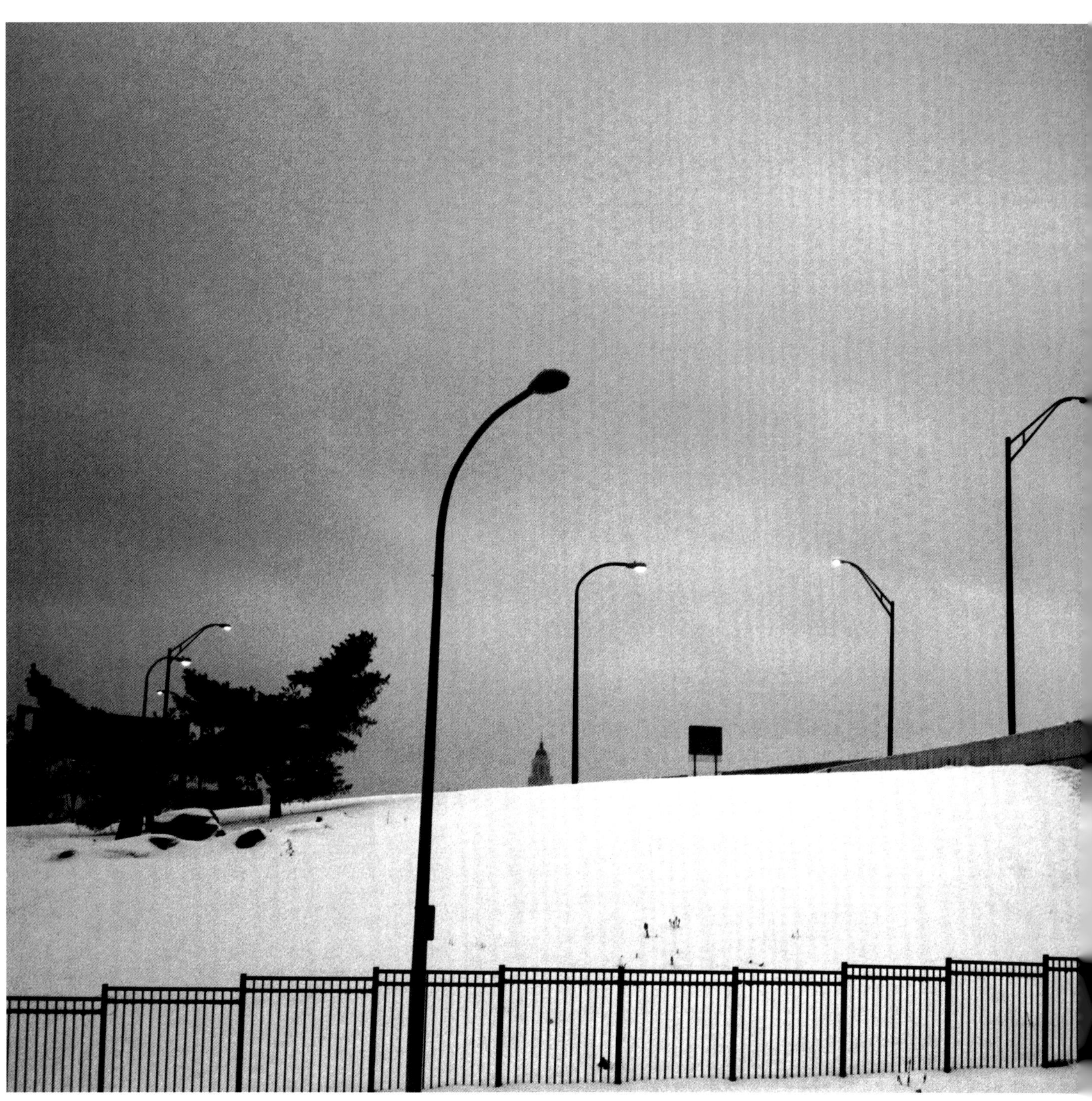

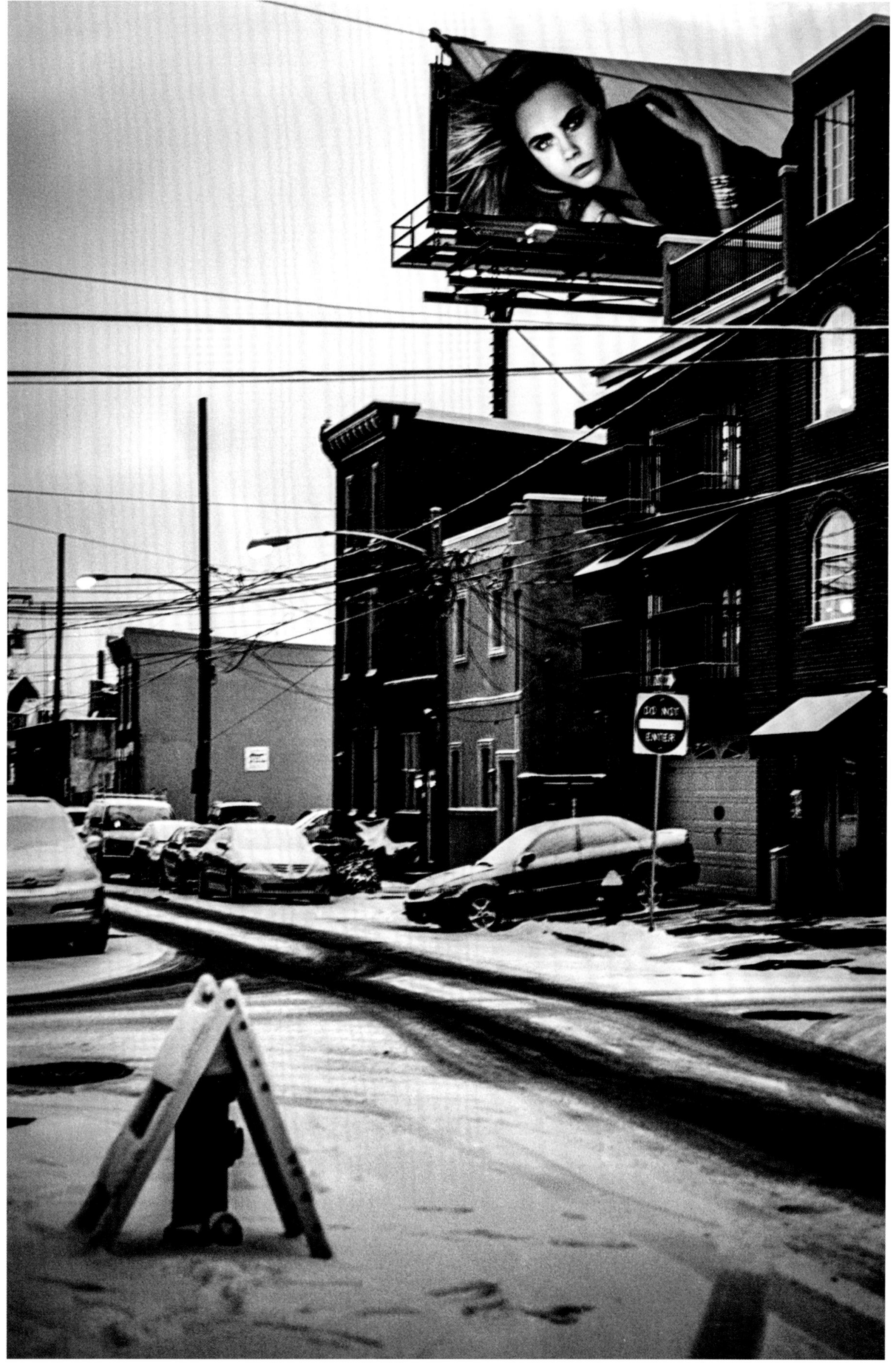

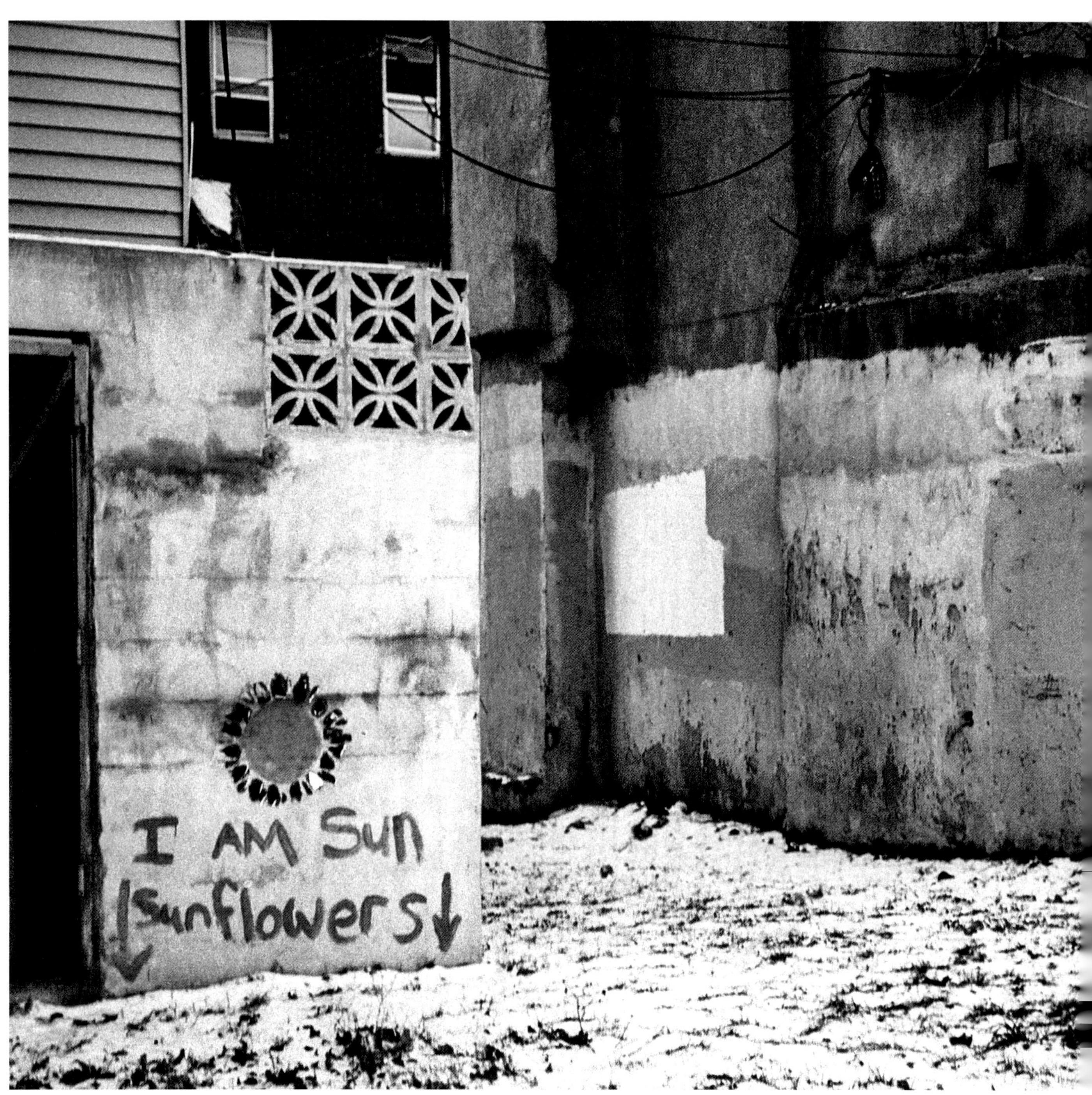

I AM Sun
Sunflowers

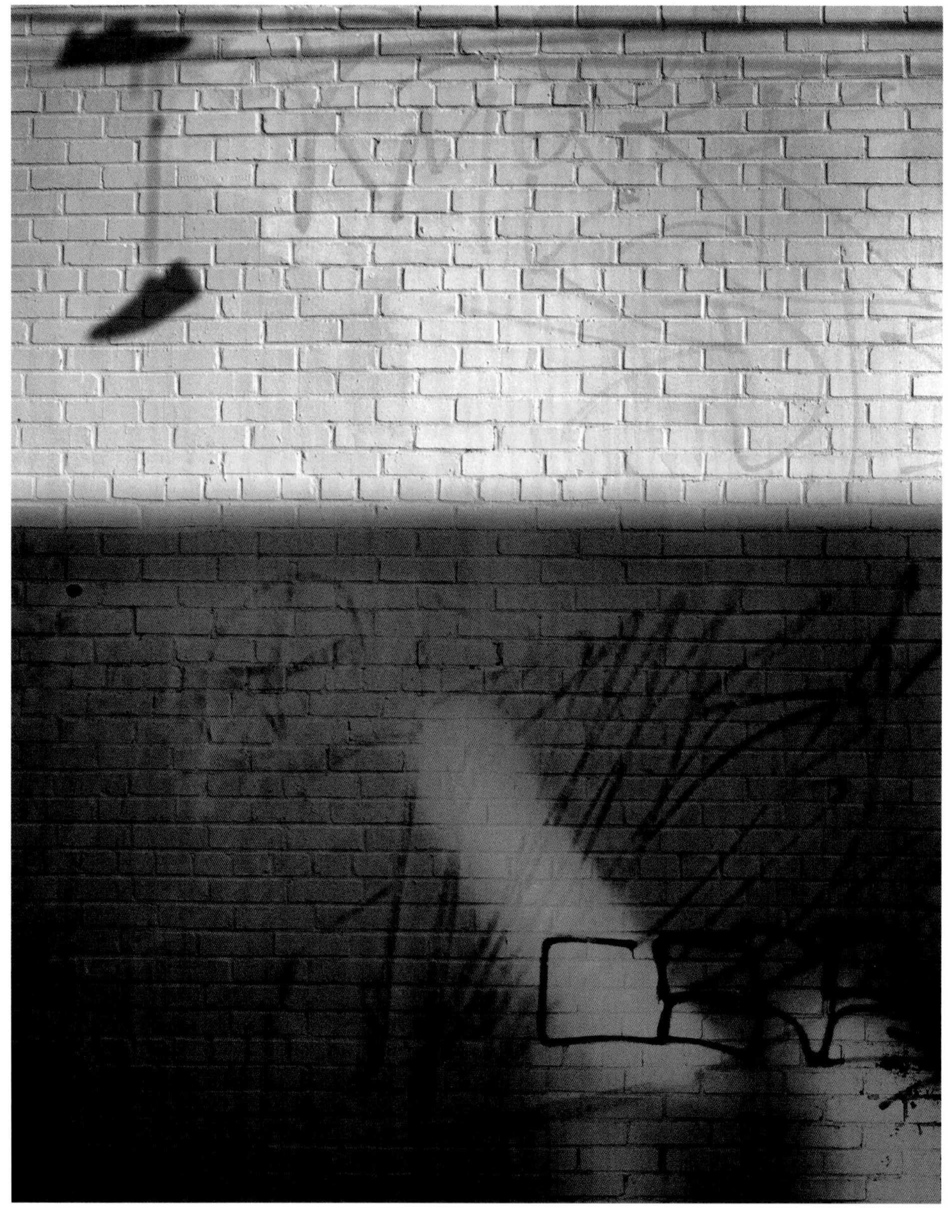

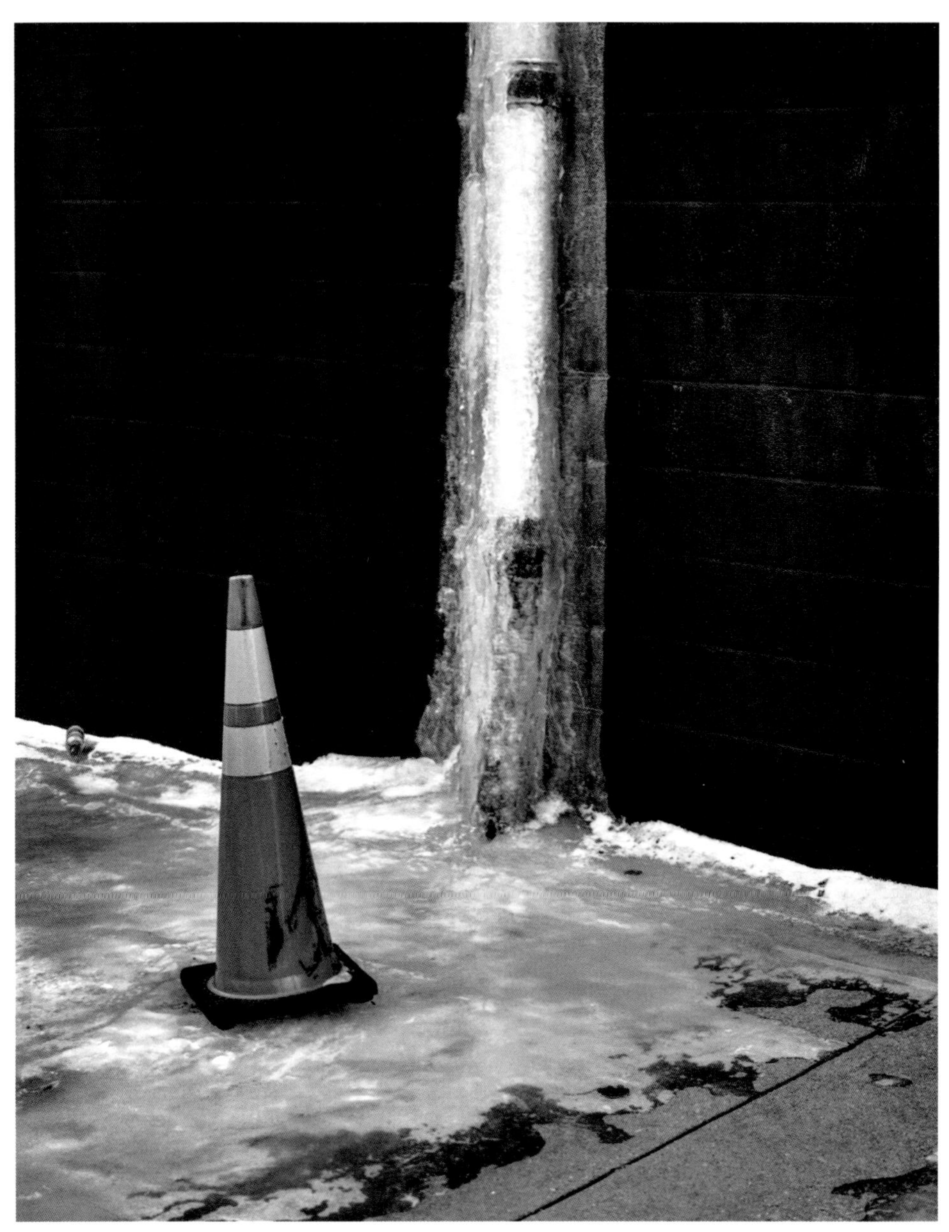

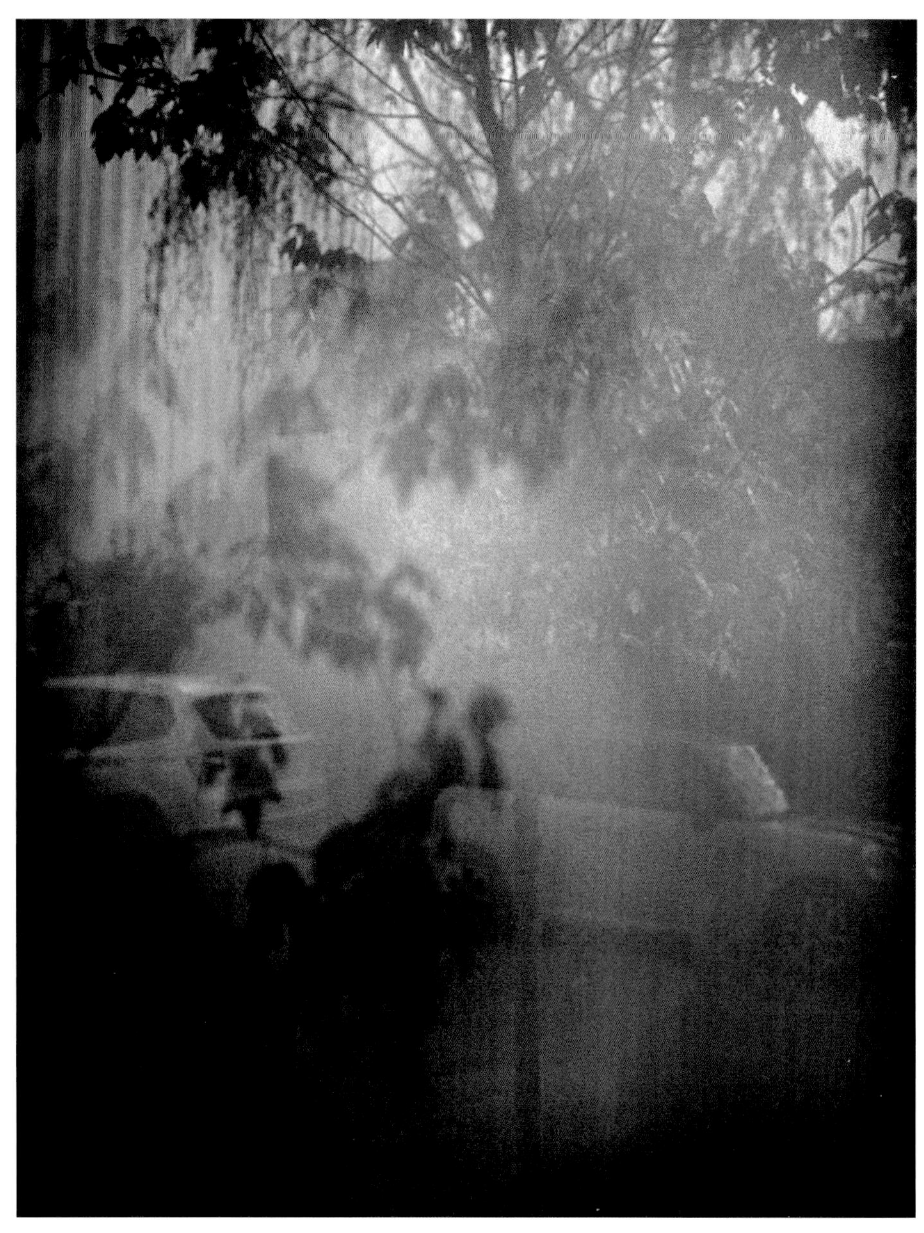

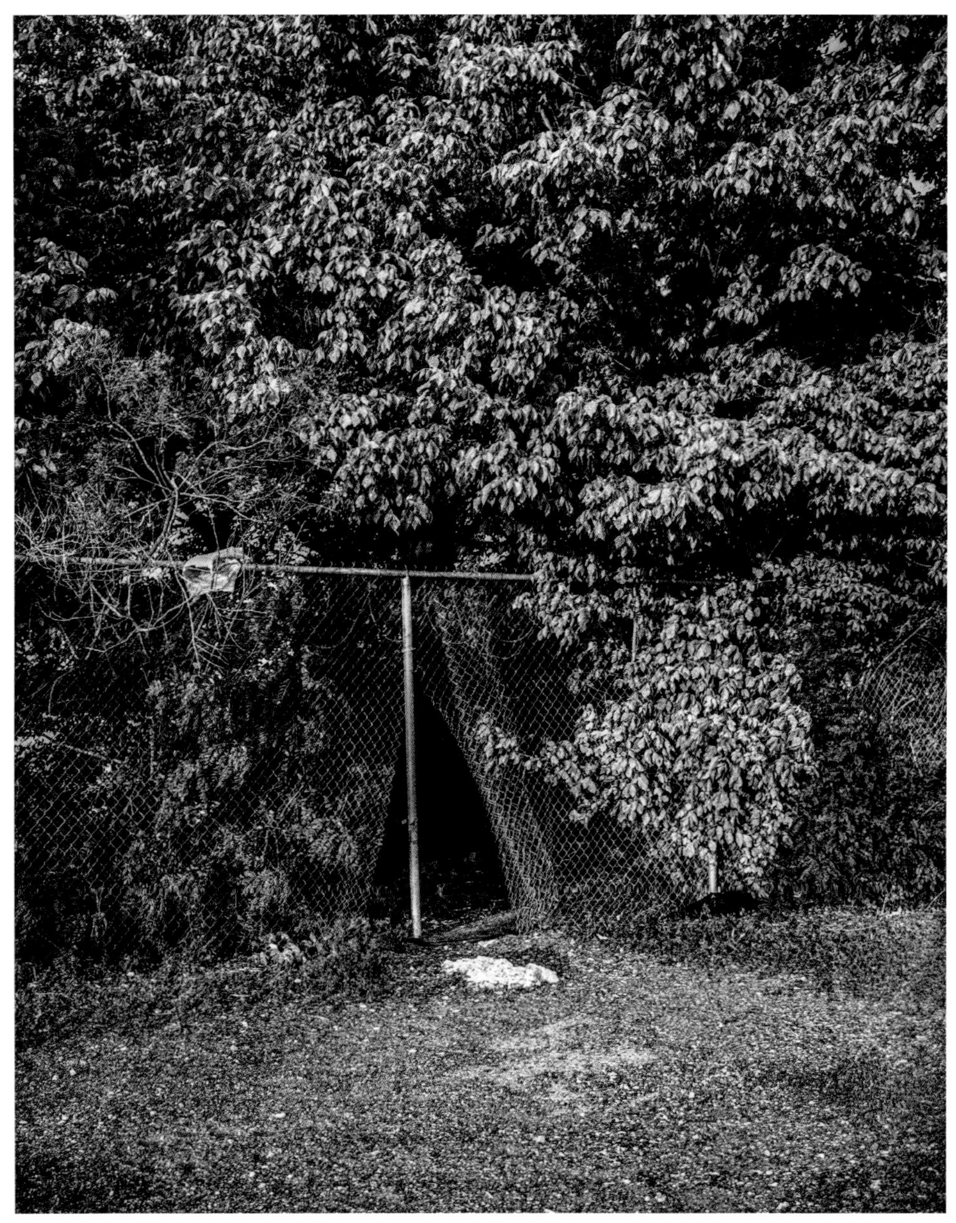

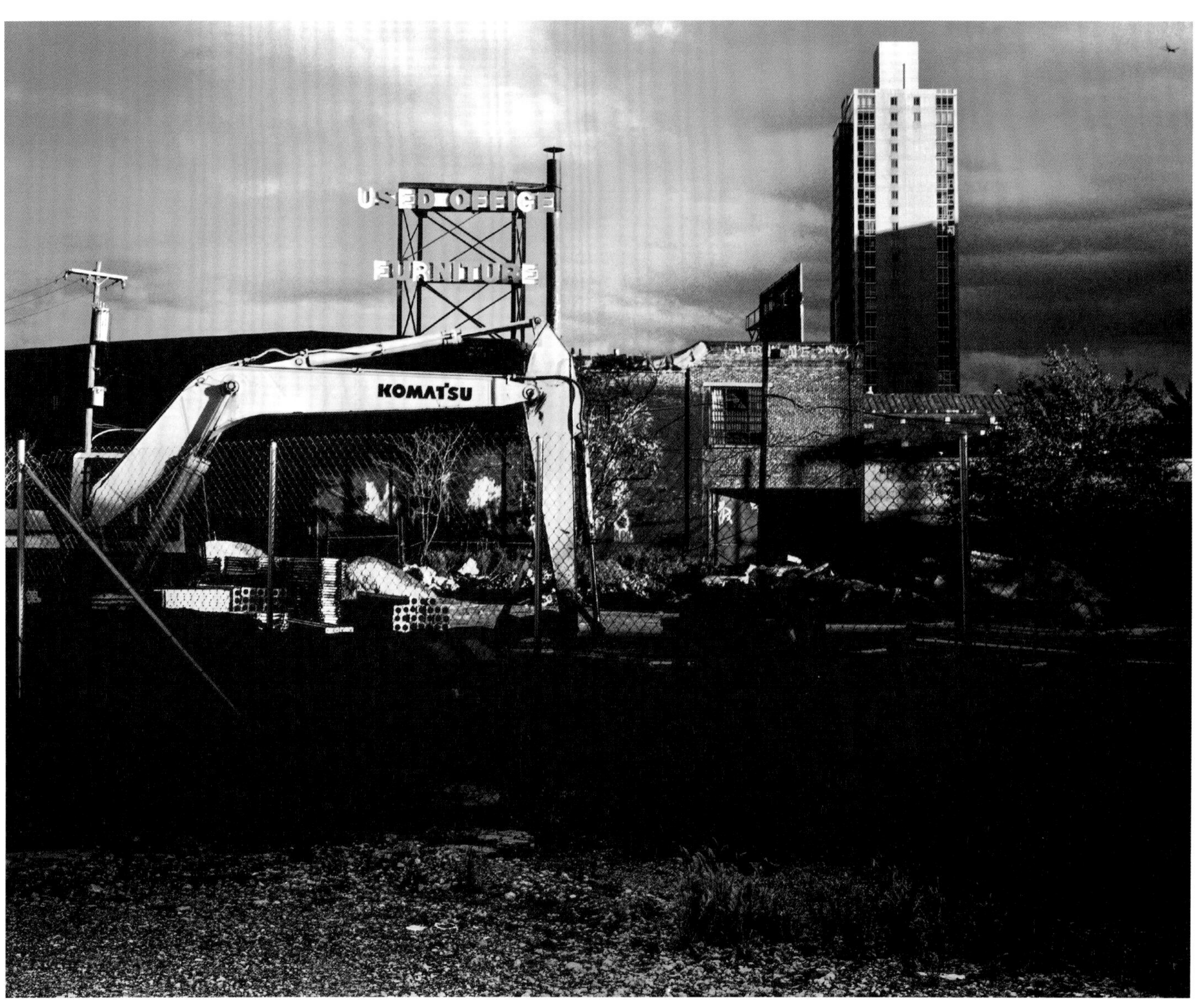

USED OFFICE
FURNITURE
KOMATSU

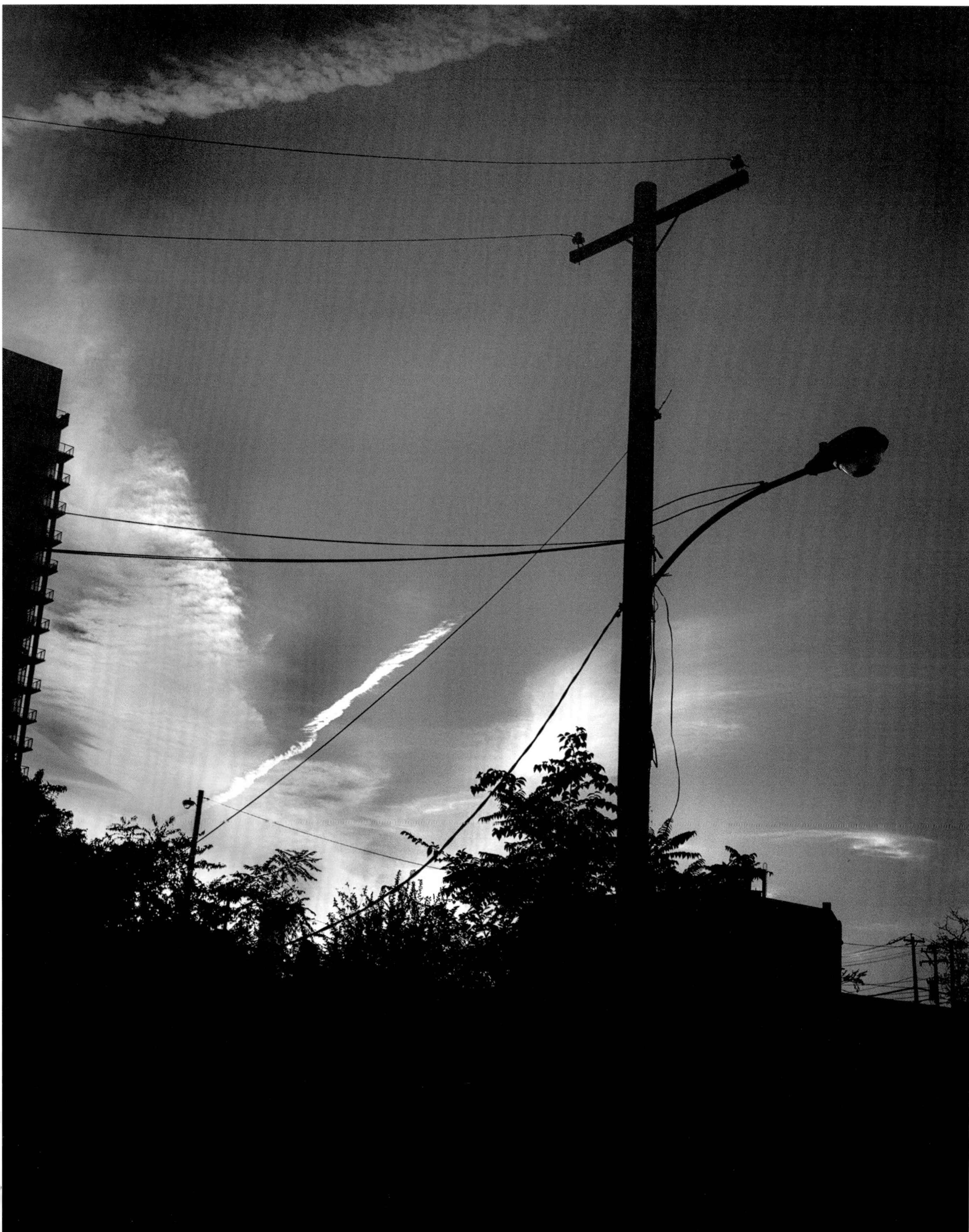

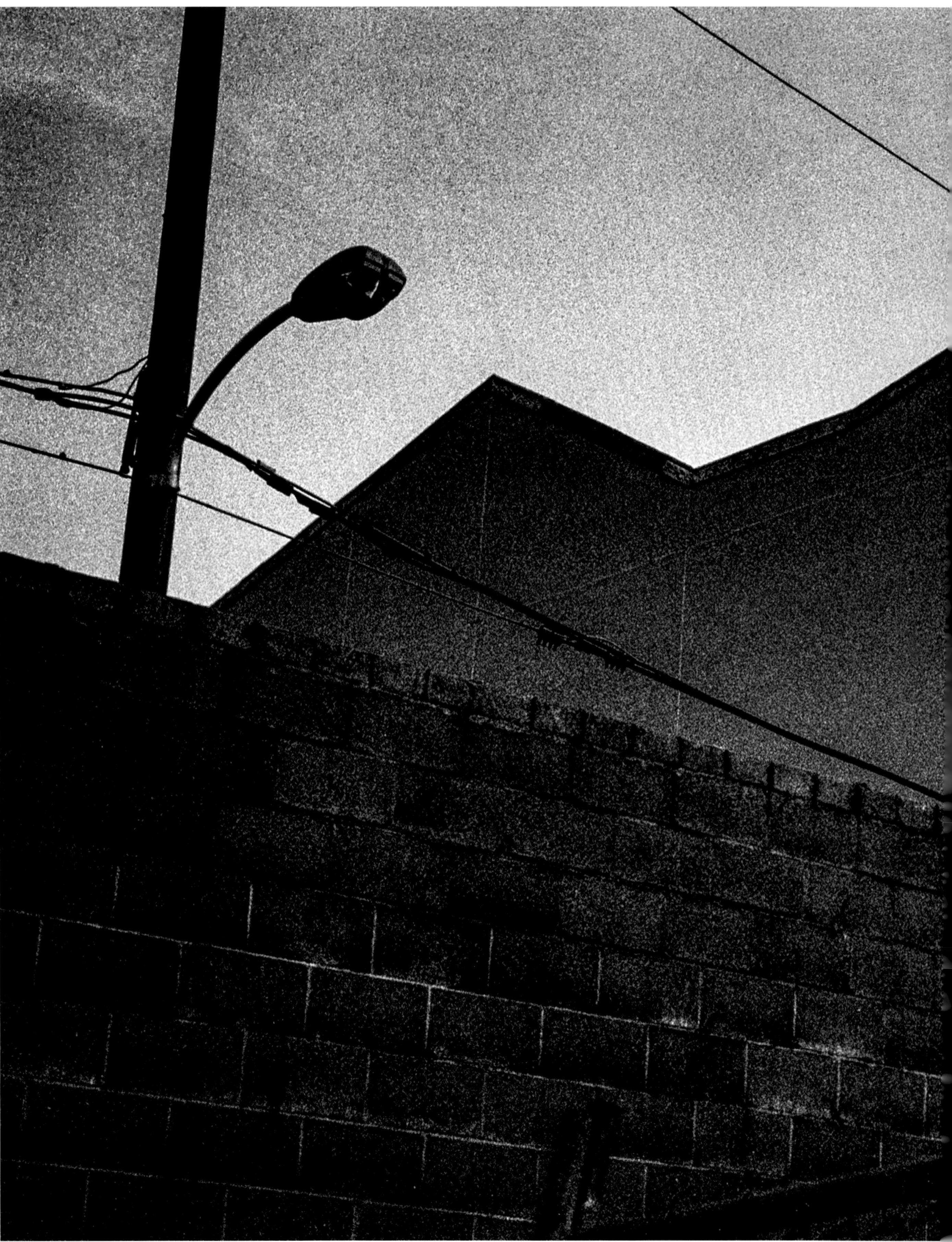

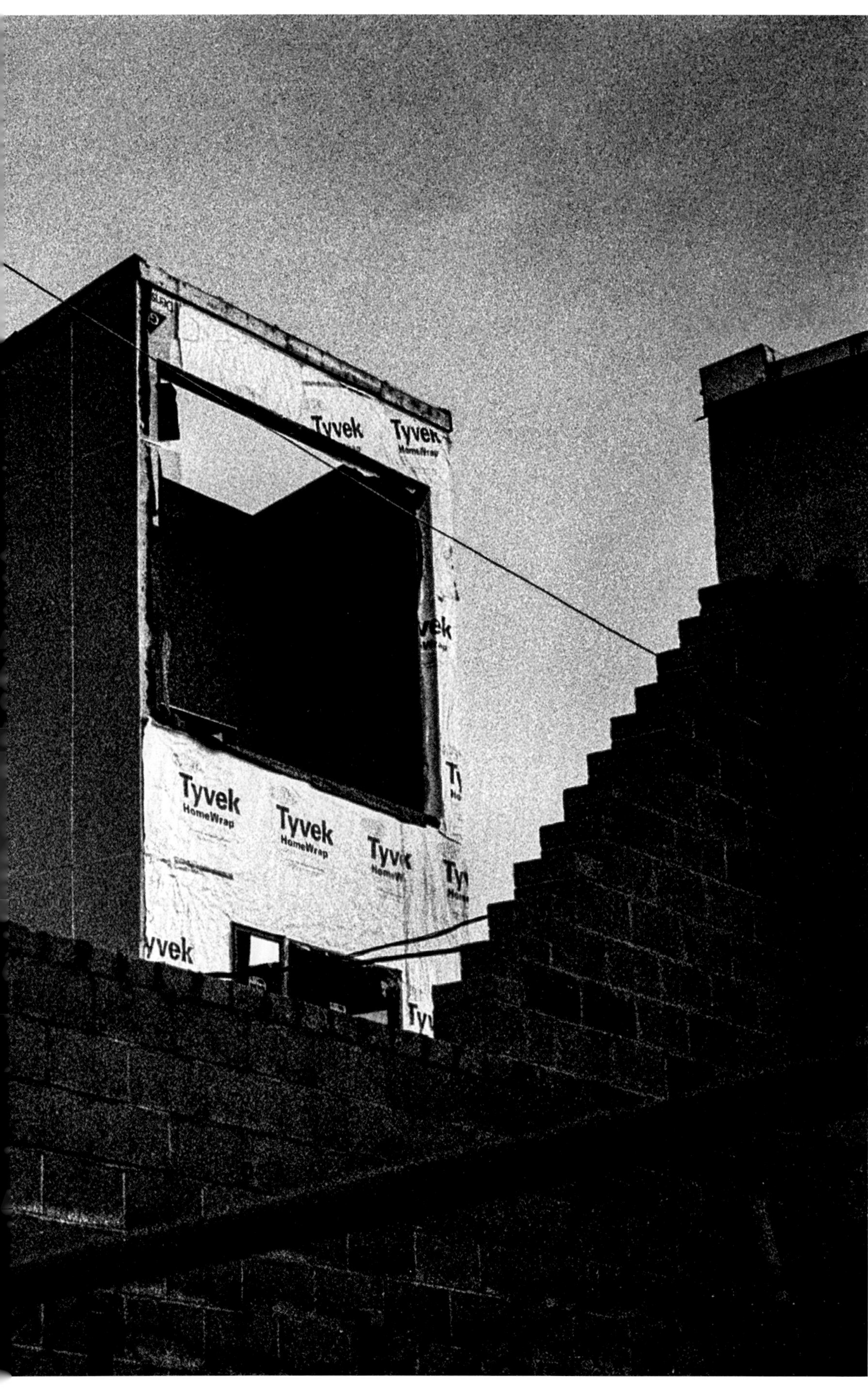

Tyvek
HomeWrap
Tyvek
HomeWrap
Tyvek
HomeWrap
Tyvek
HomeWrap
Tyvek
Tyvek

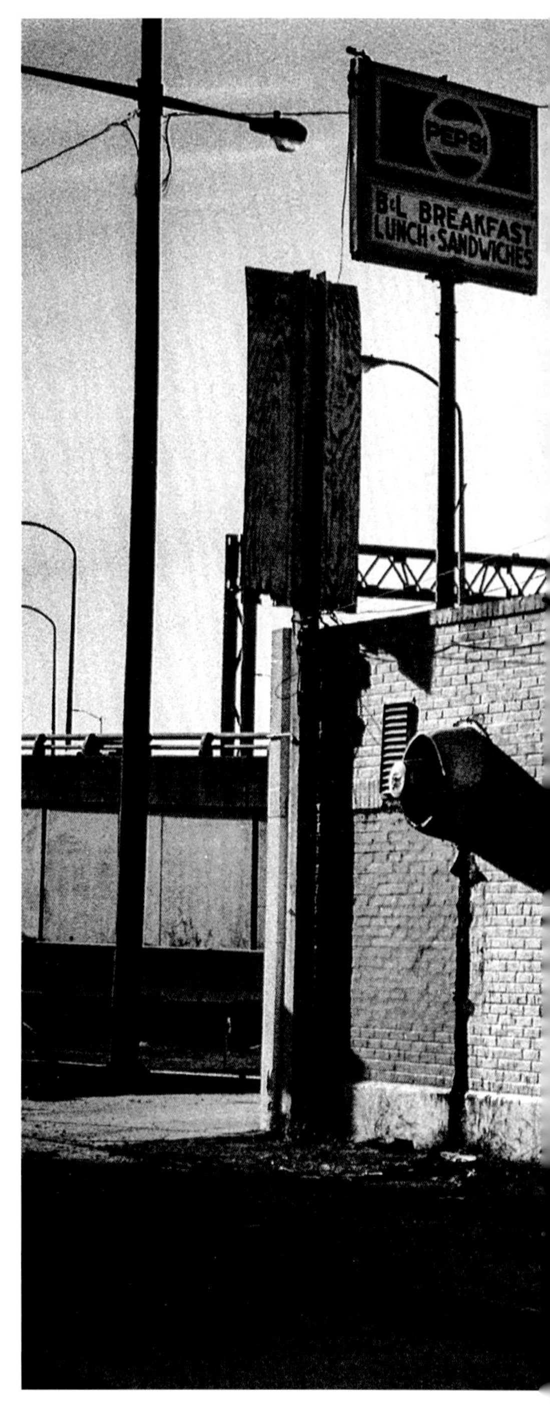
PEPSI
B&L BREAKFAST
LUNCH • SANDWICHES

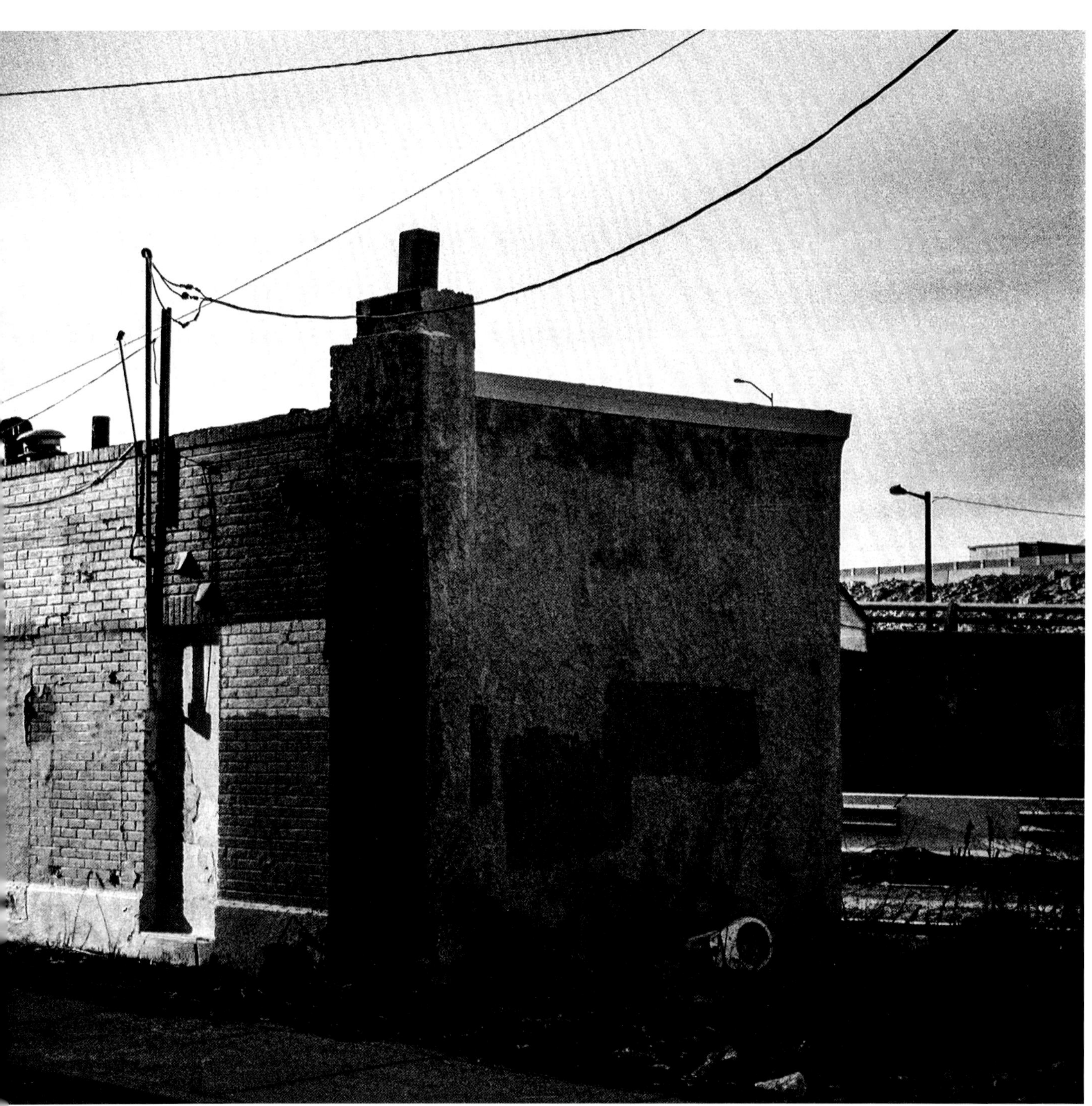

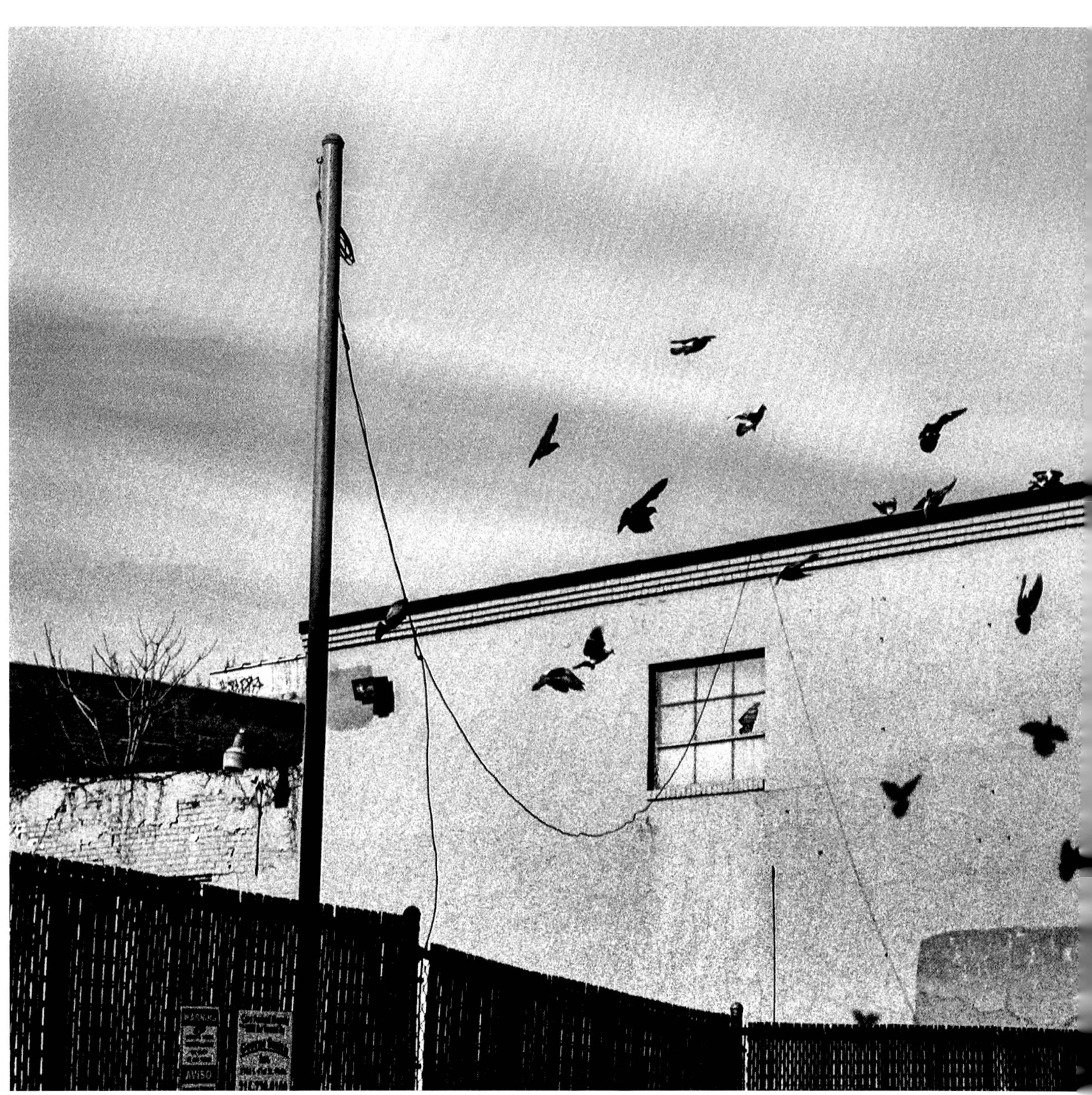

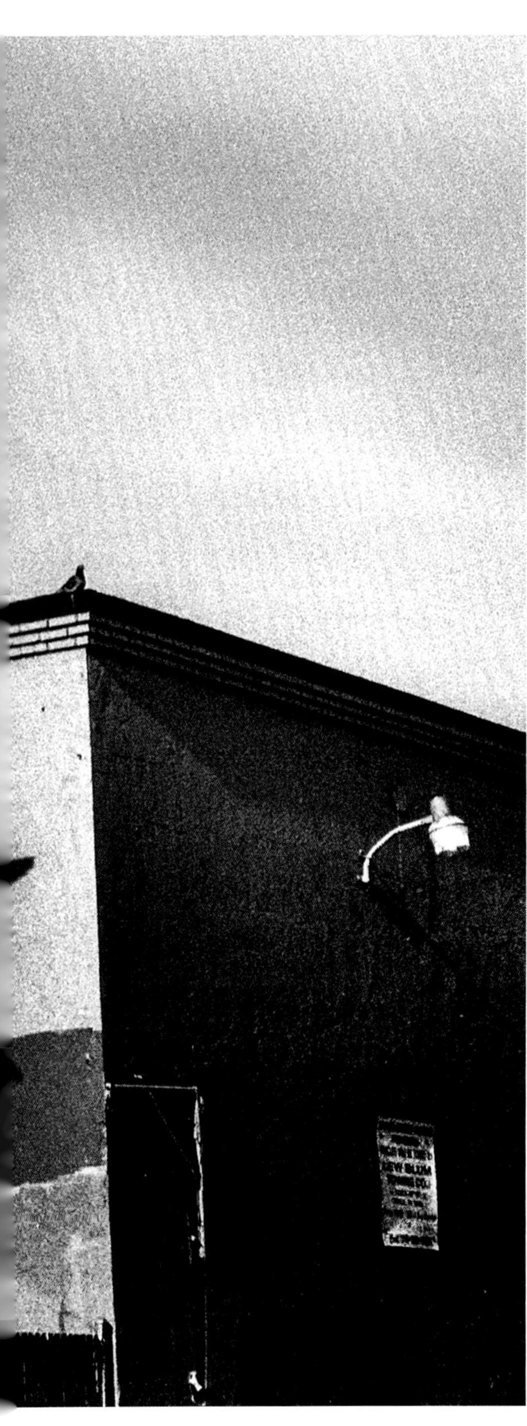

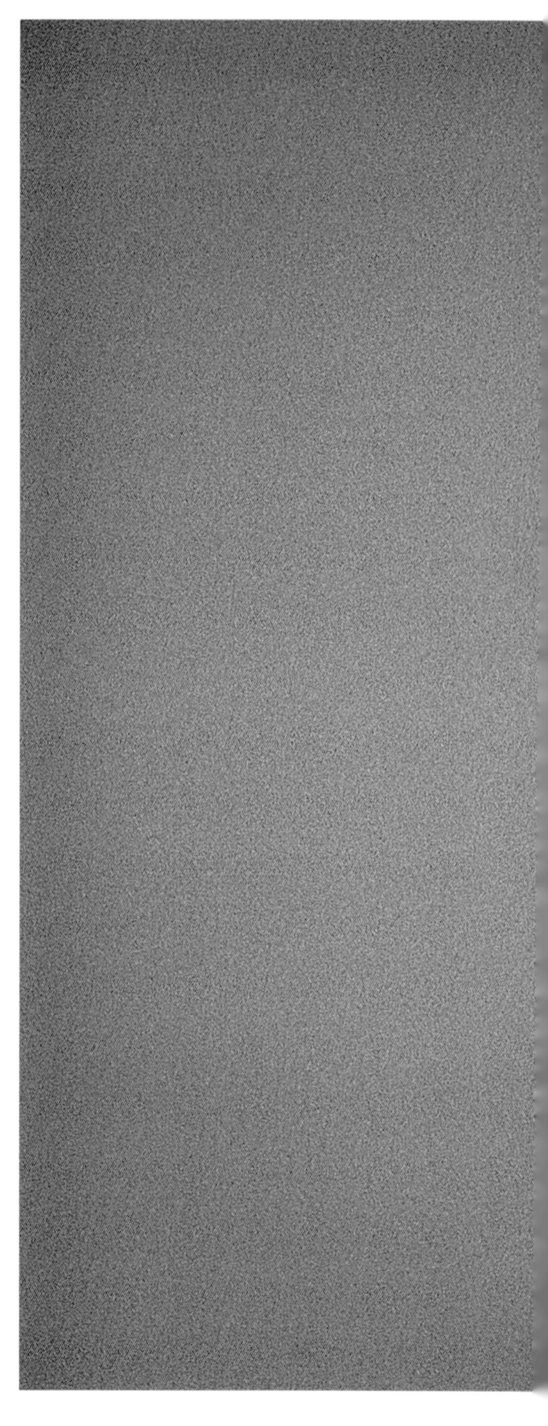

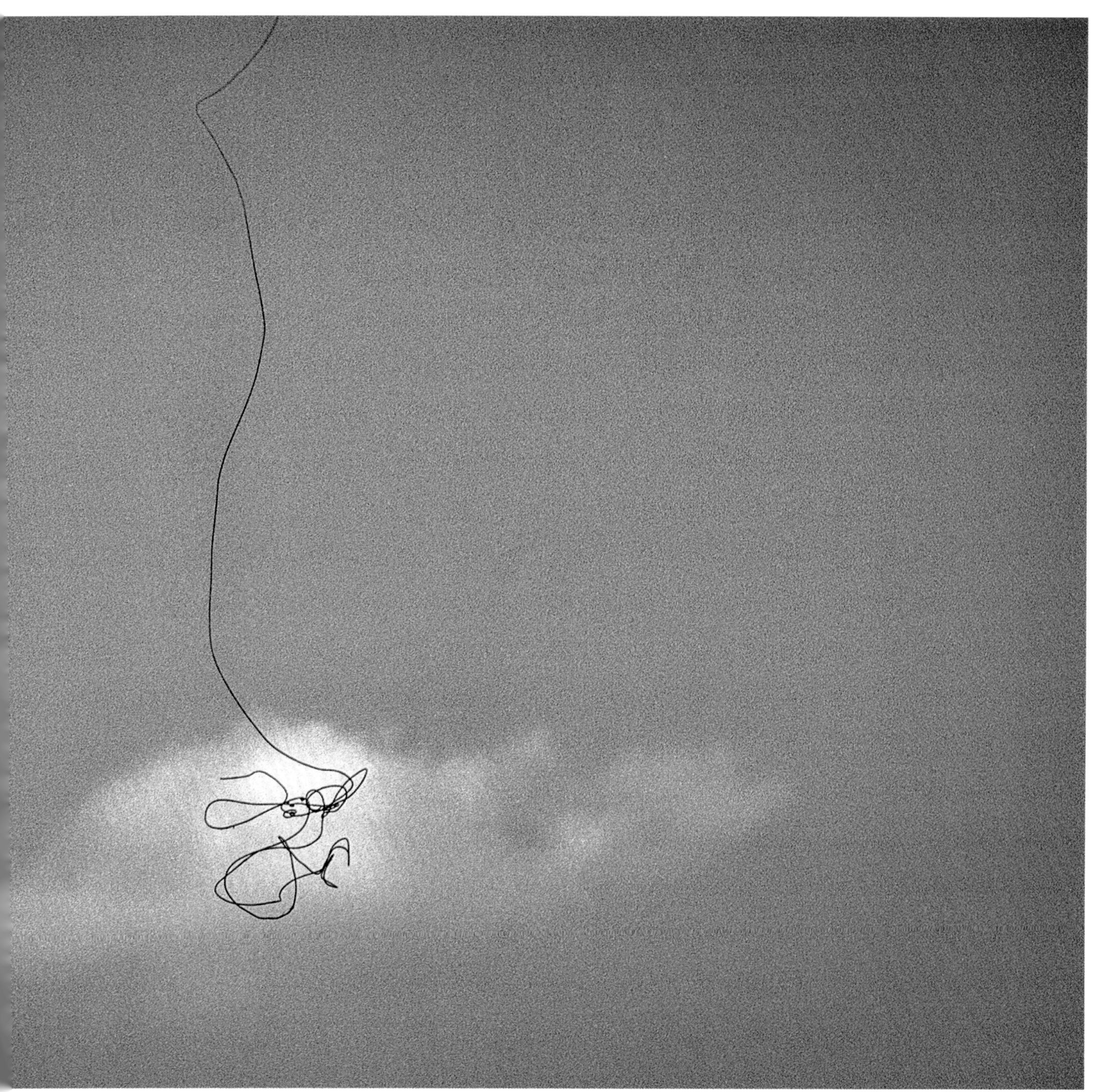

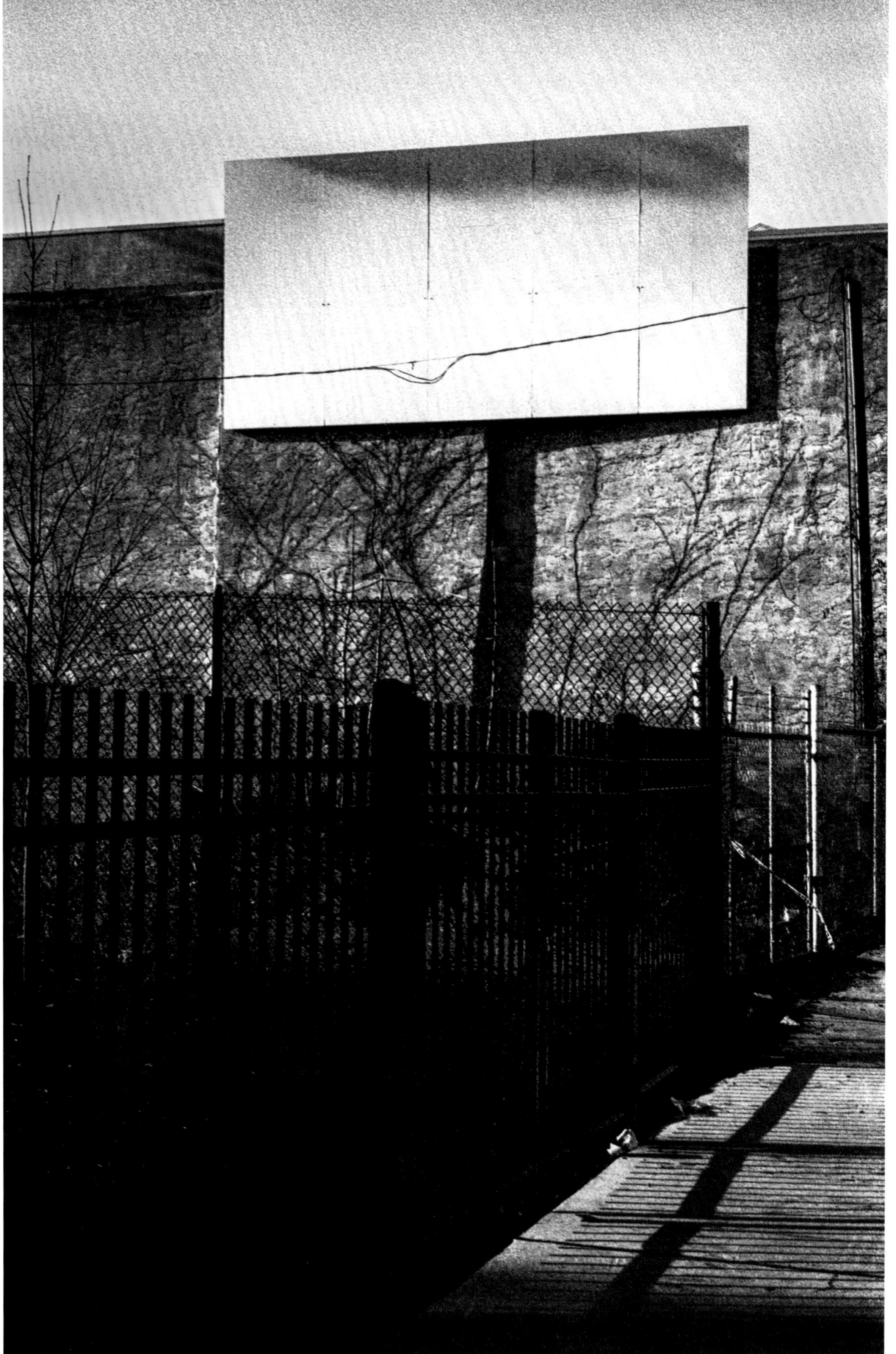

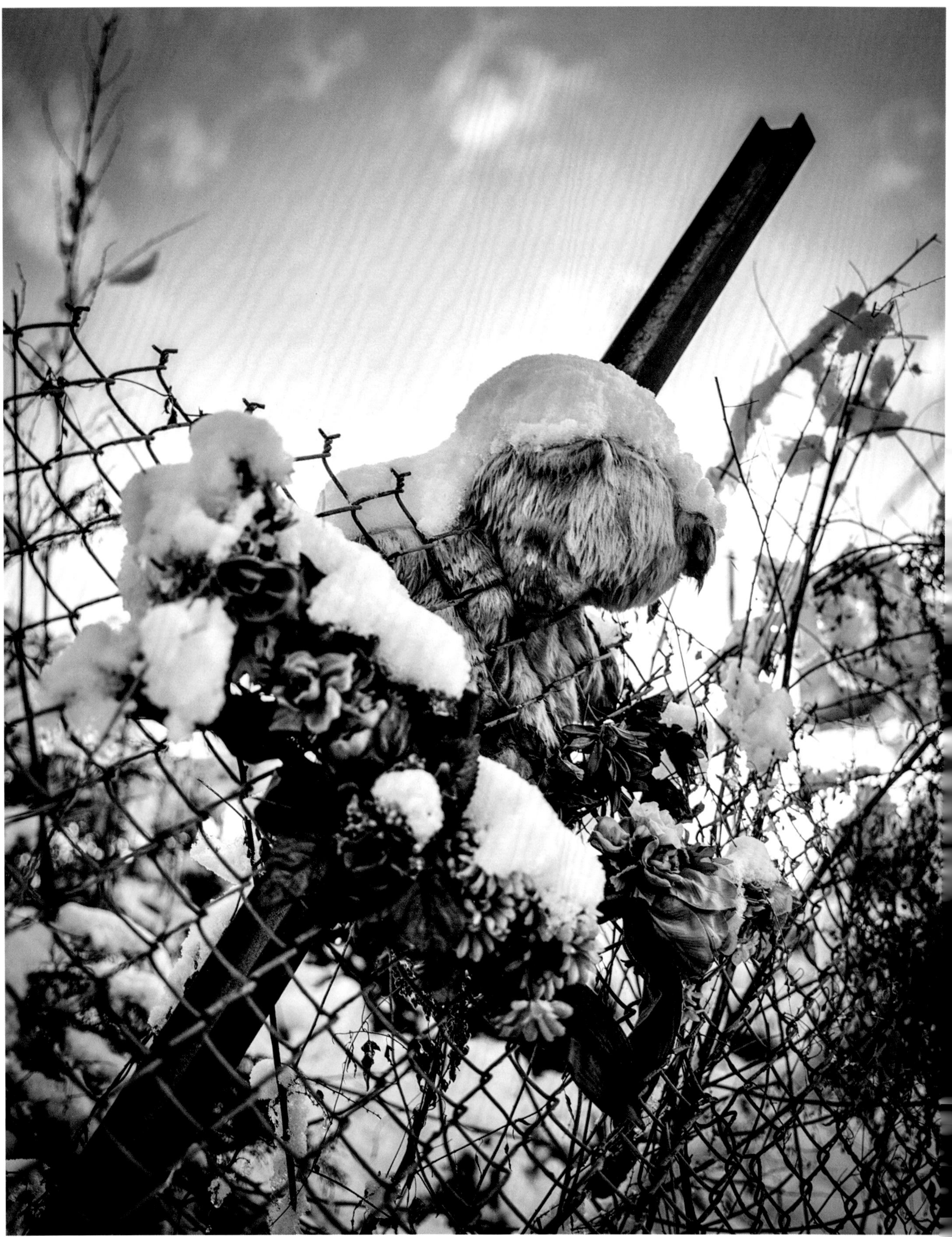

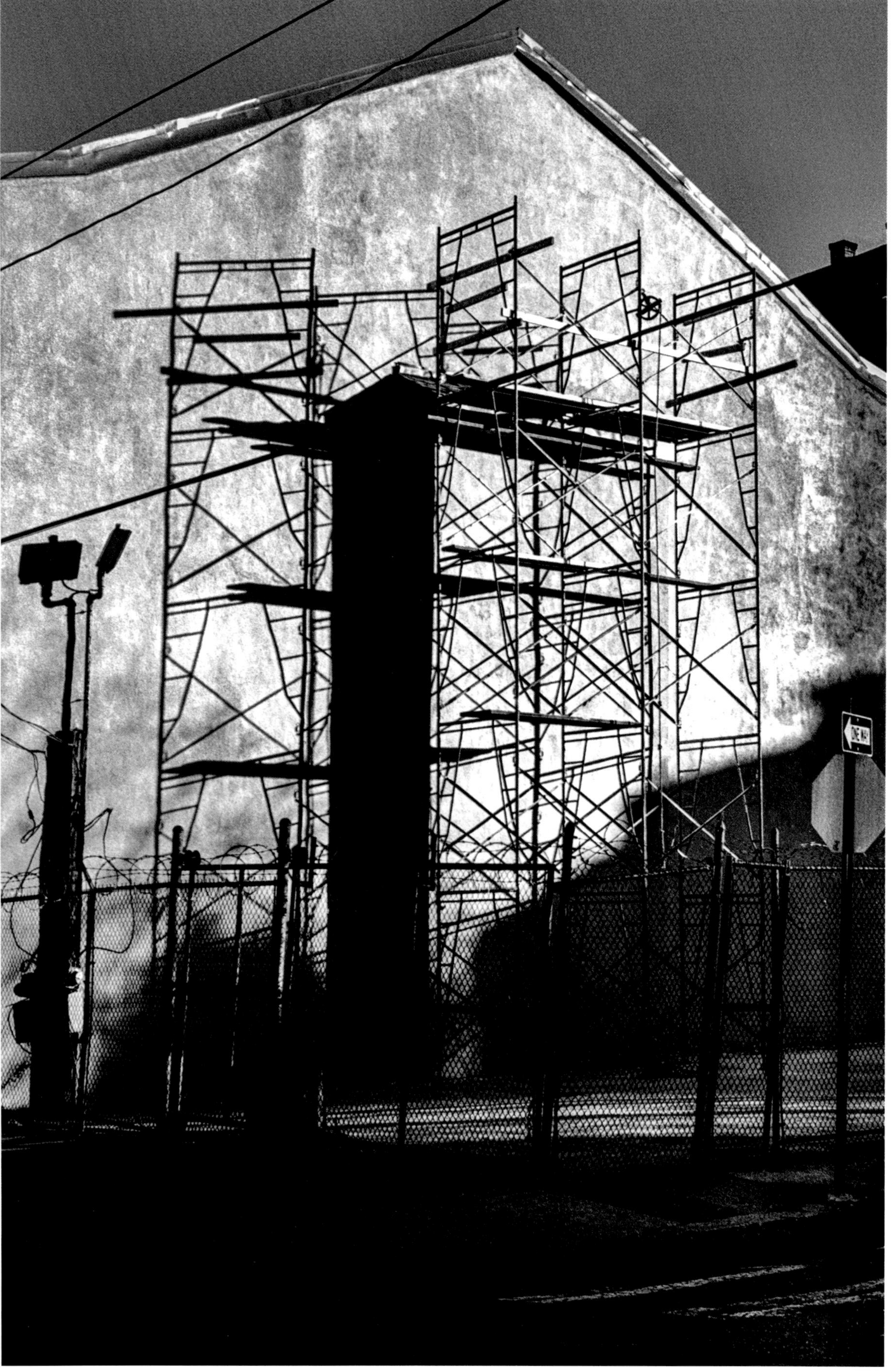

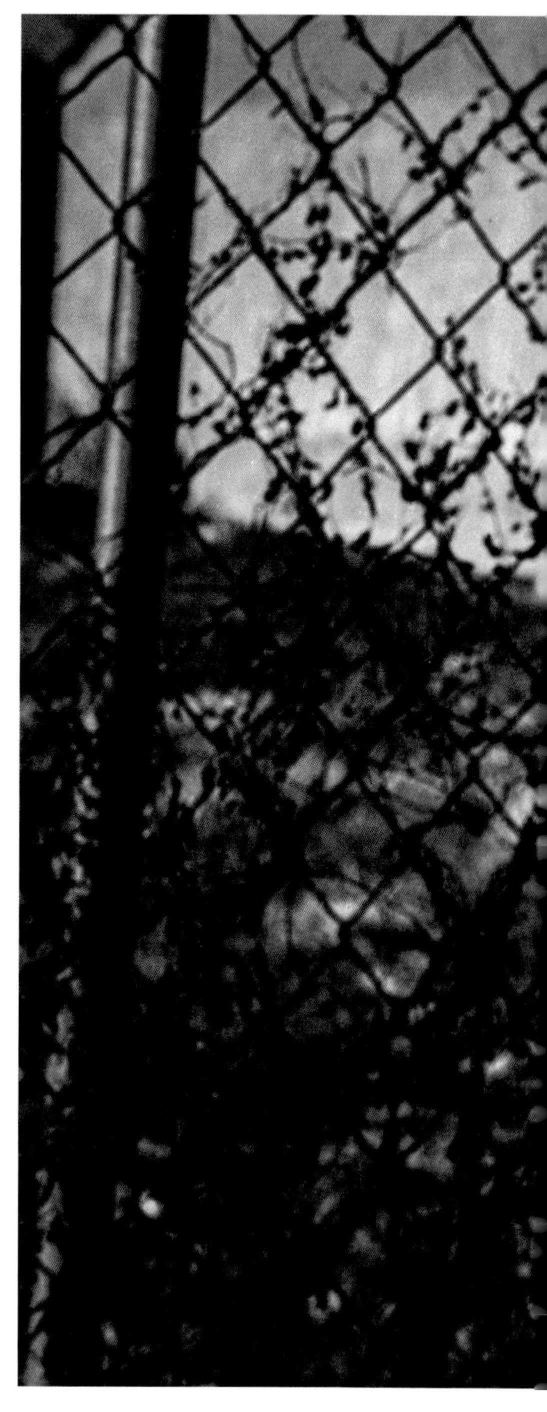

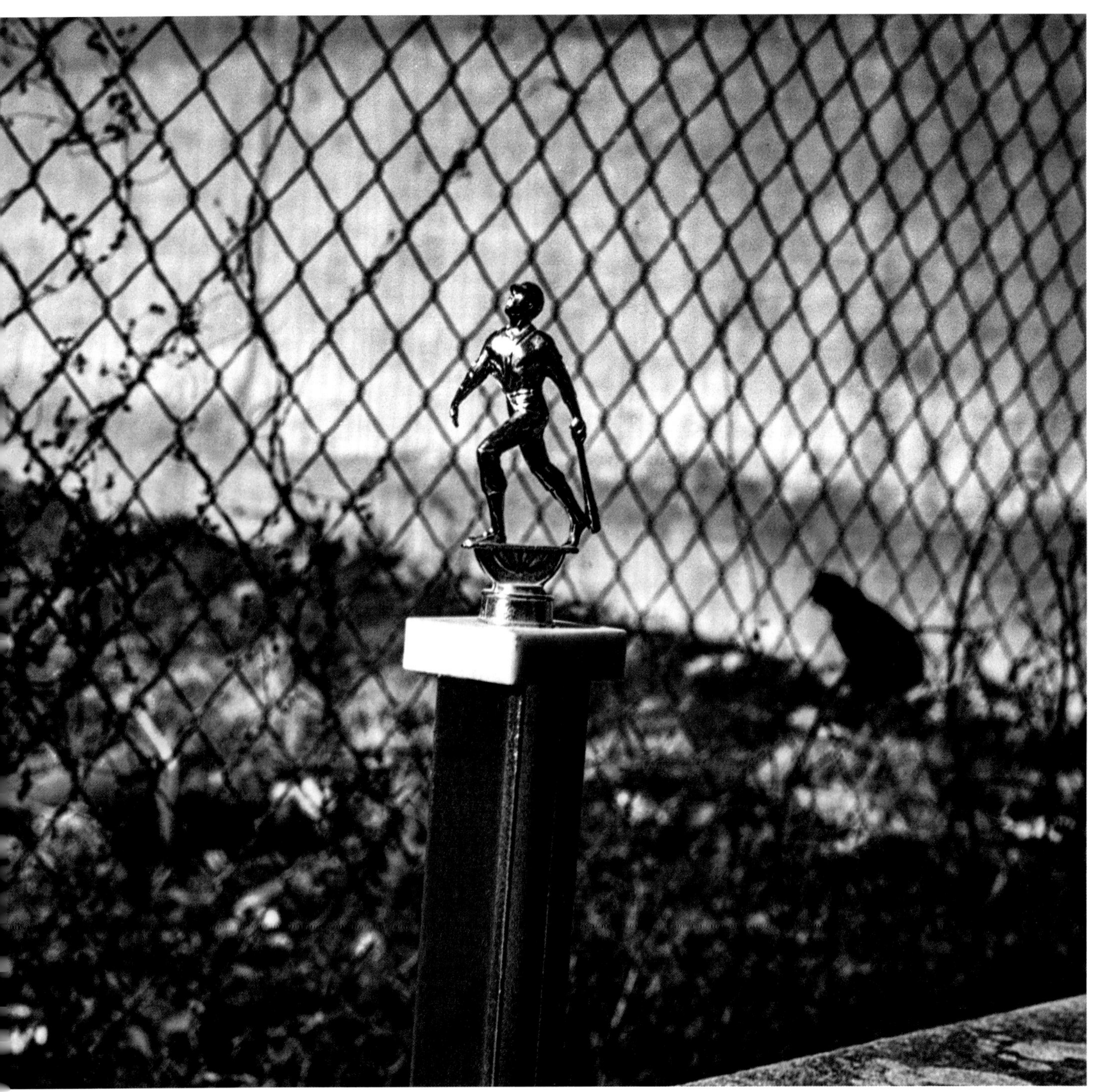

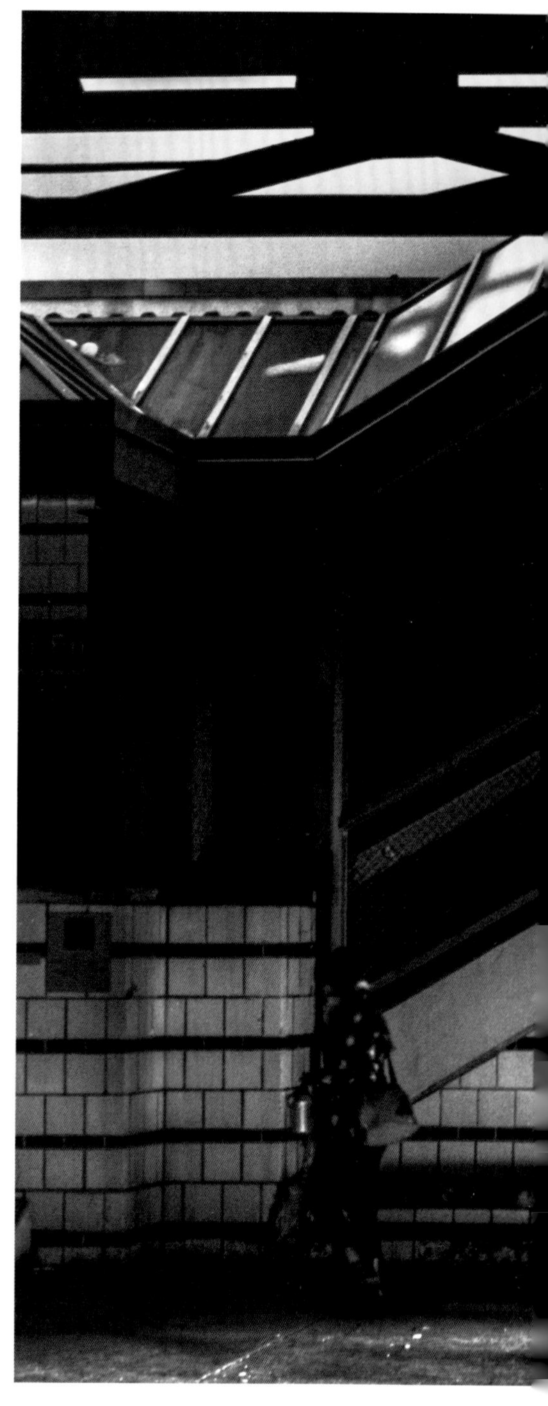

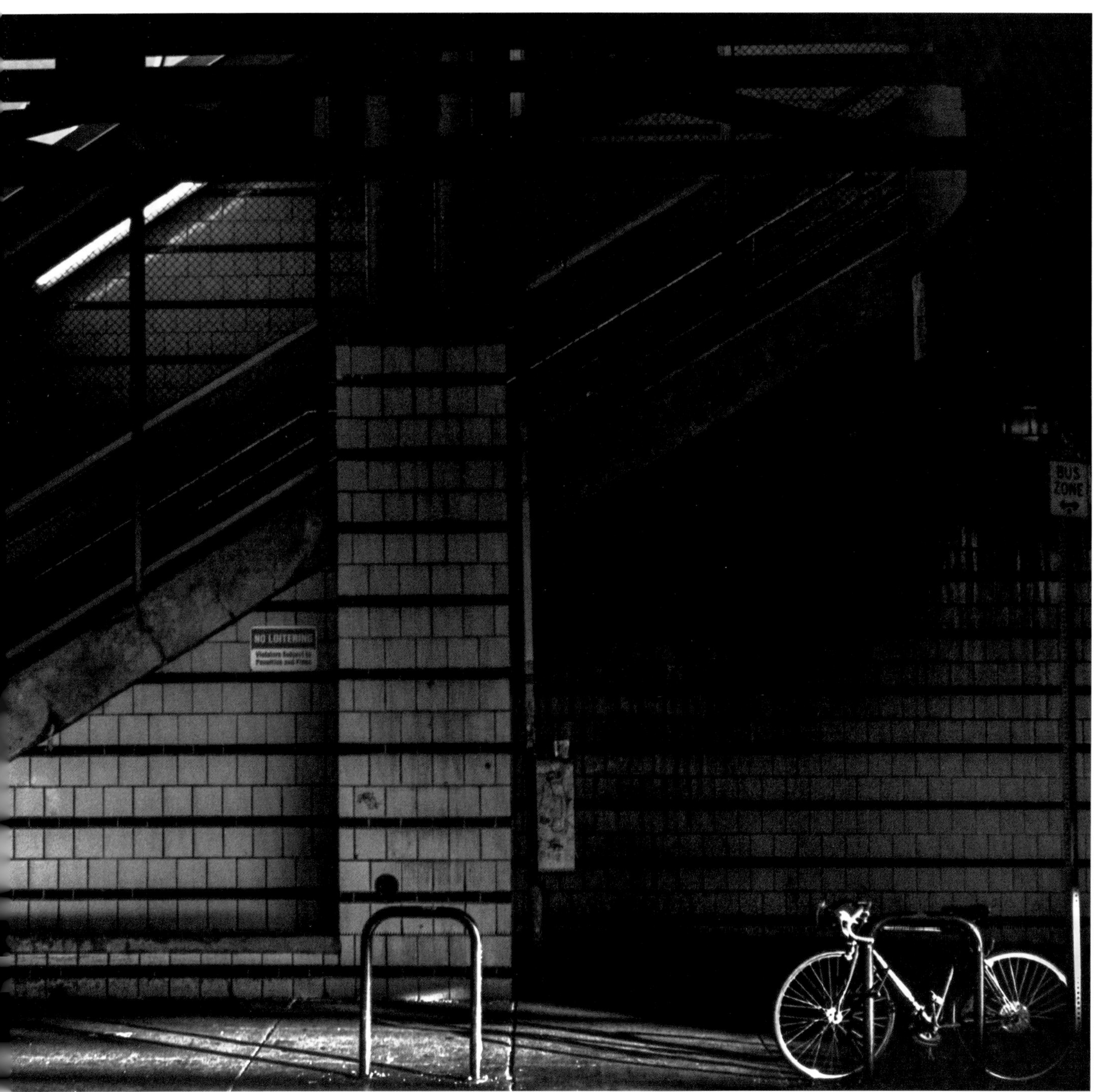
NO LOITERING
BUS
ZONE

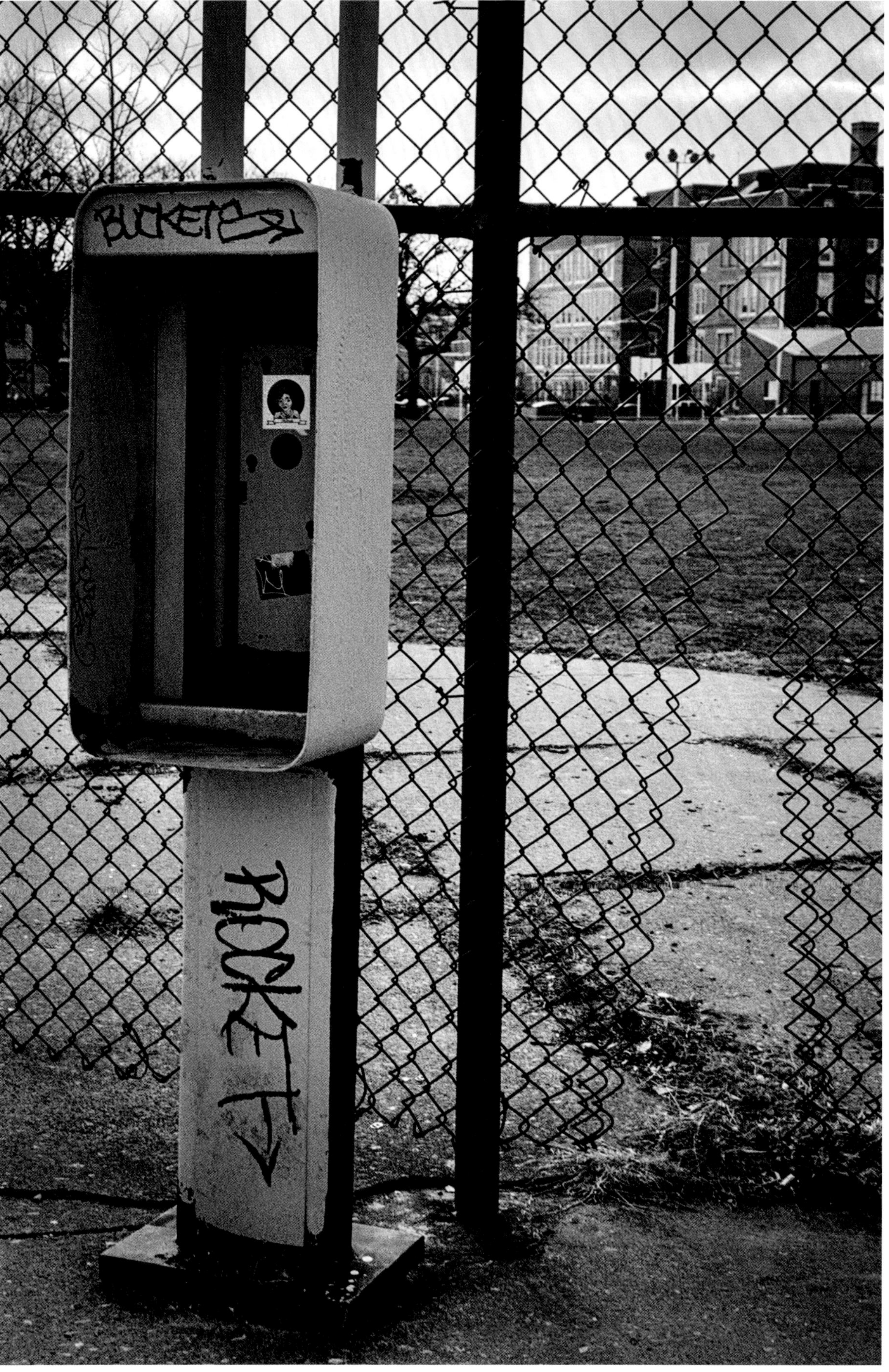
BUCKET
ROCKET

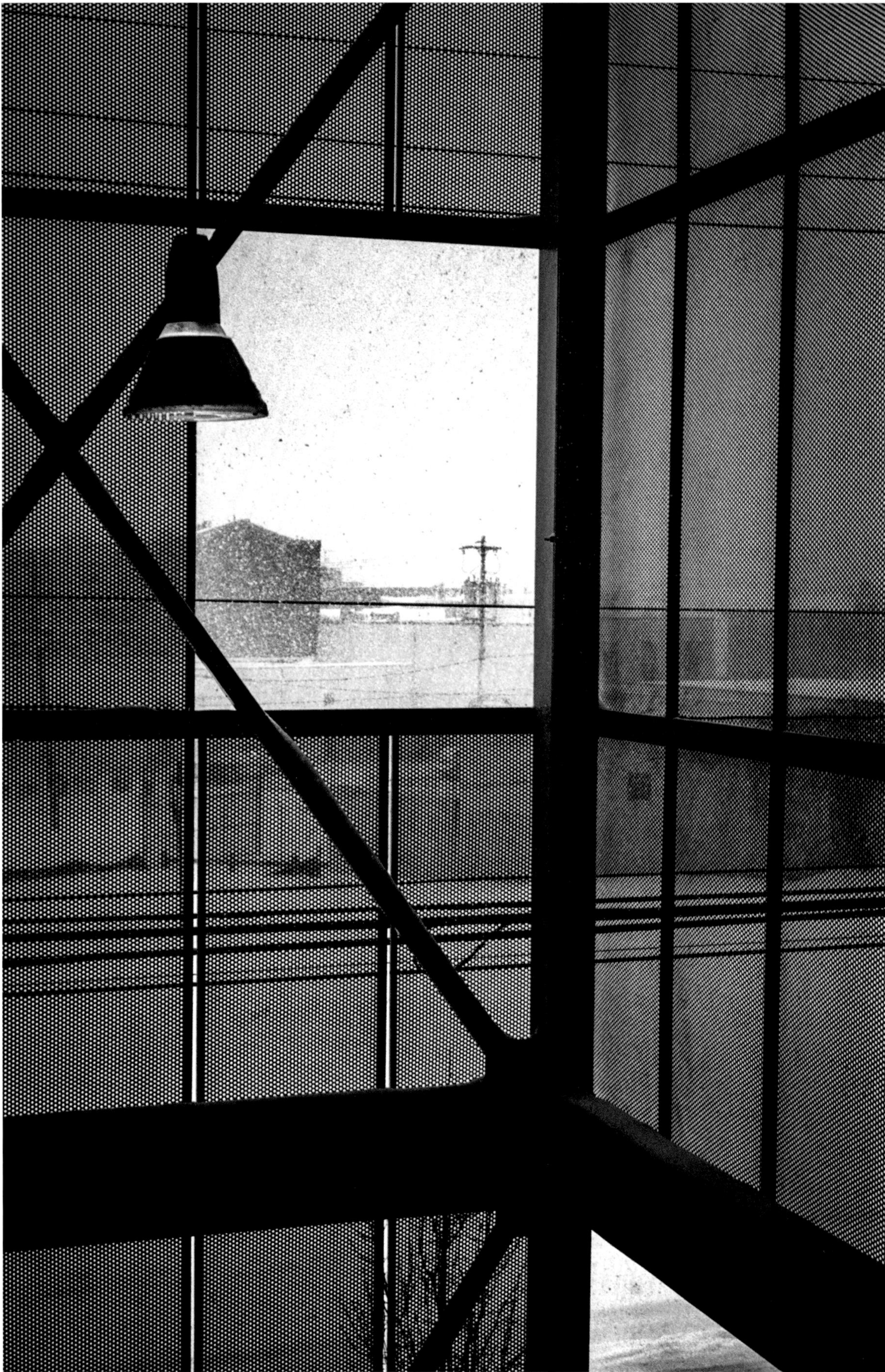

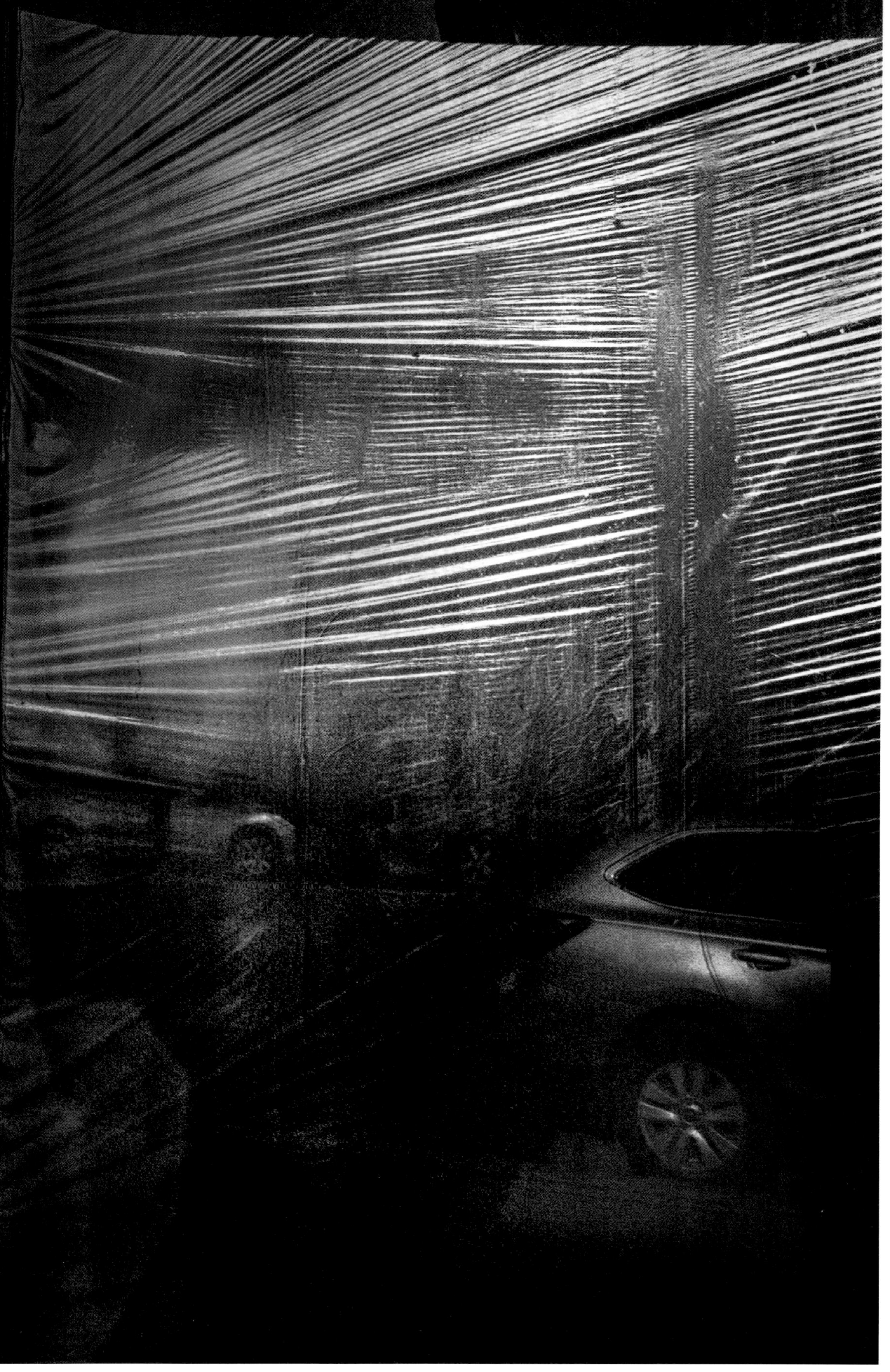

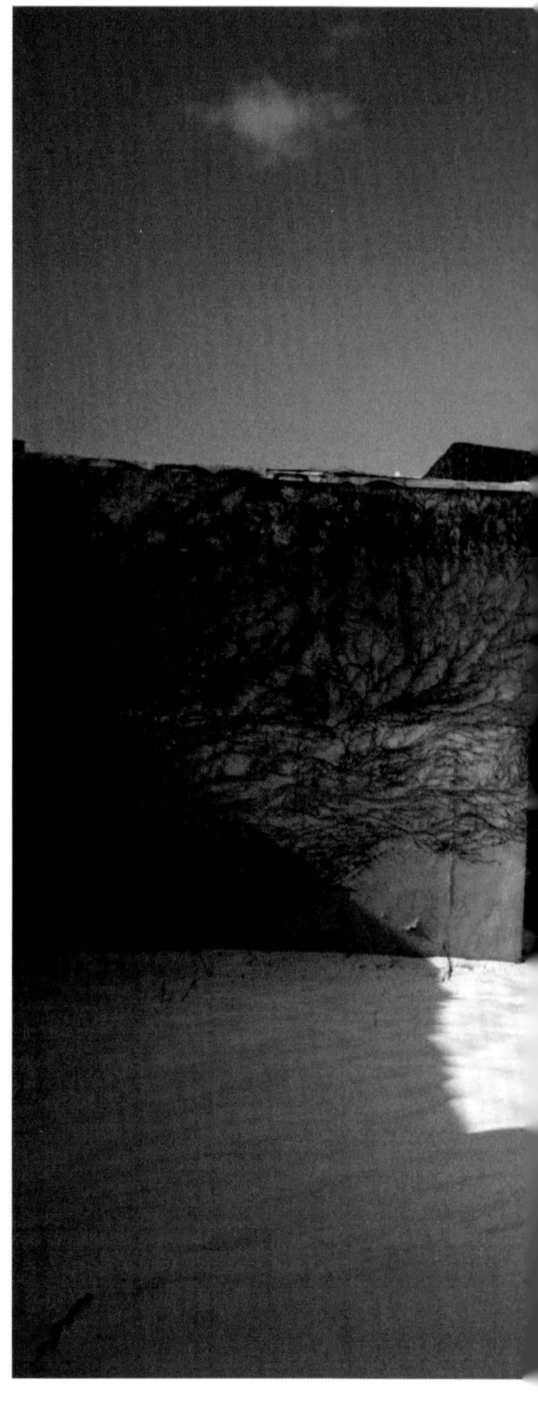

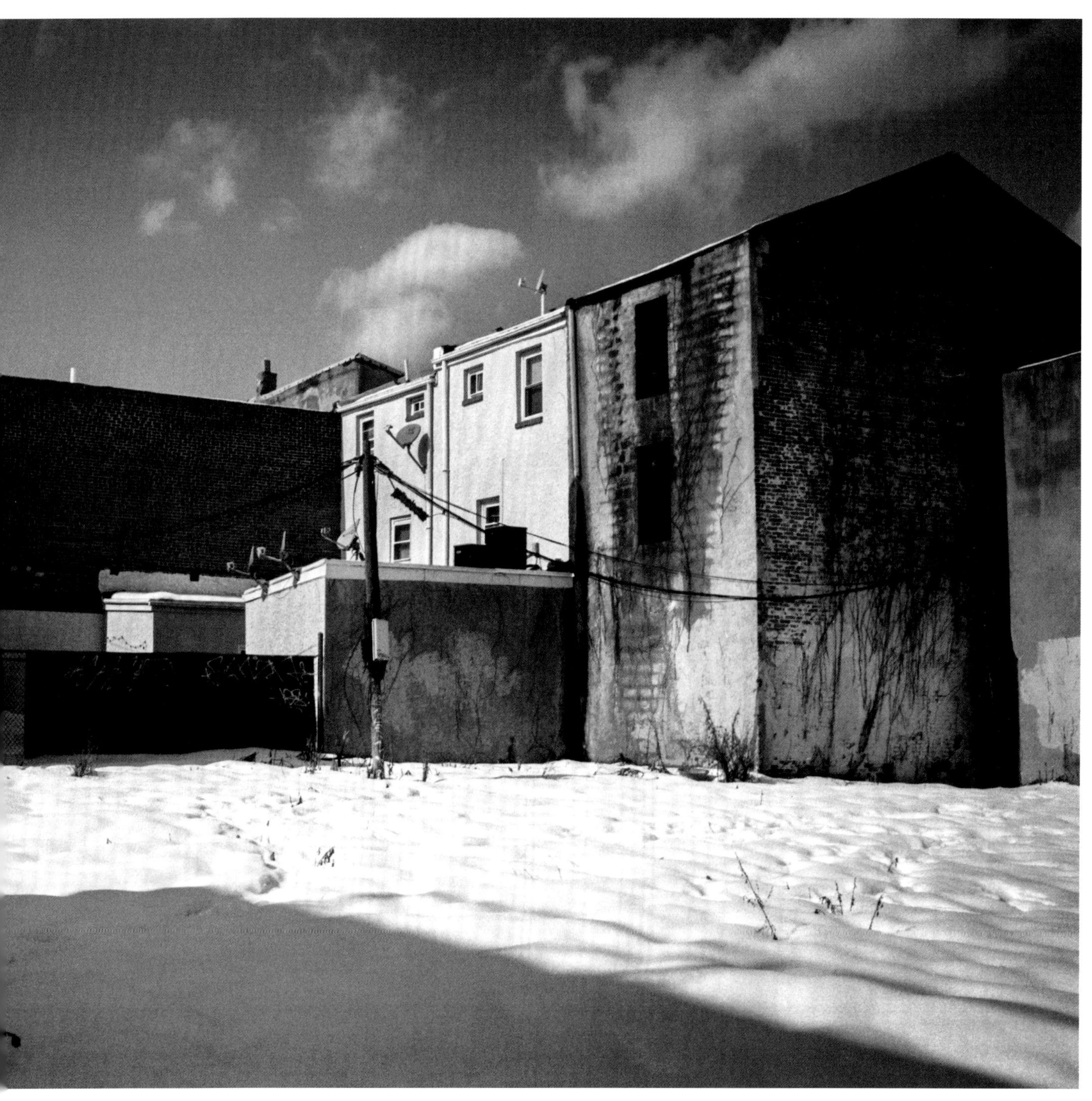

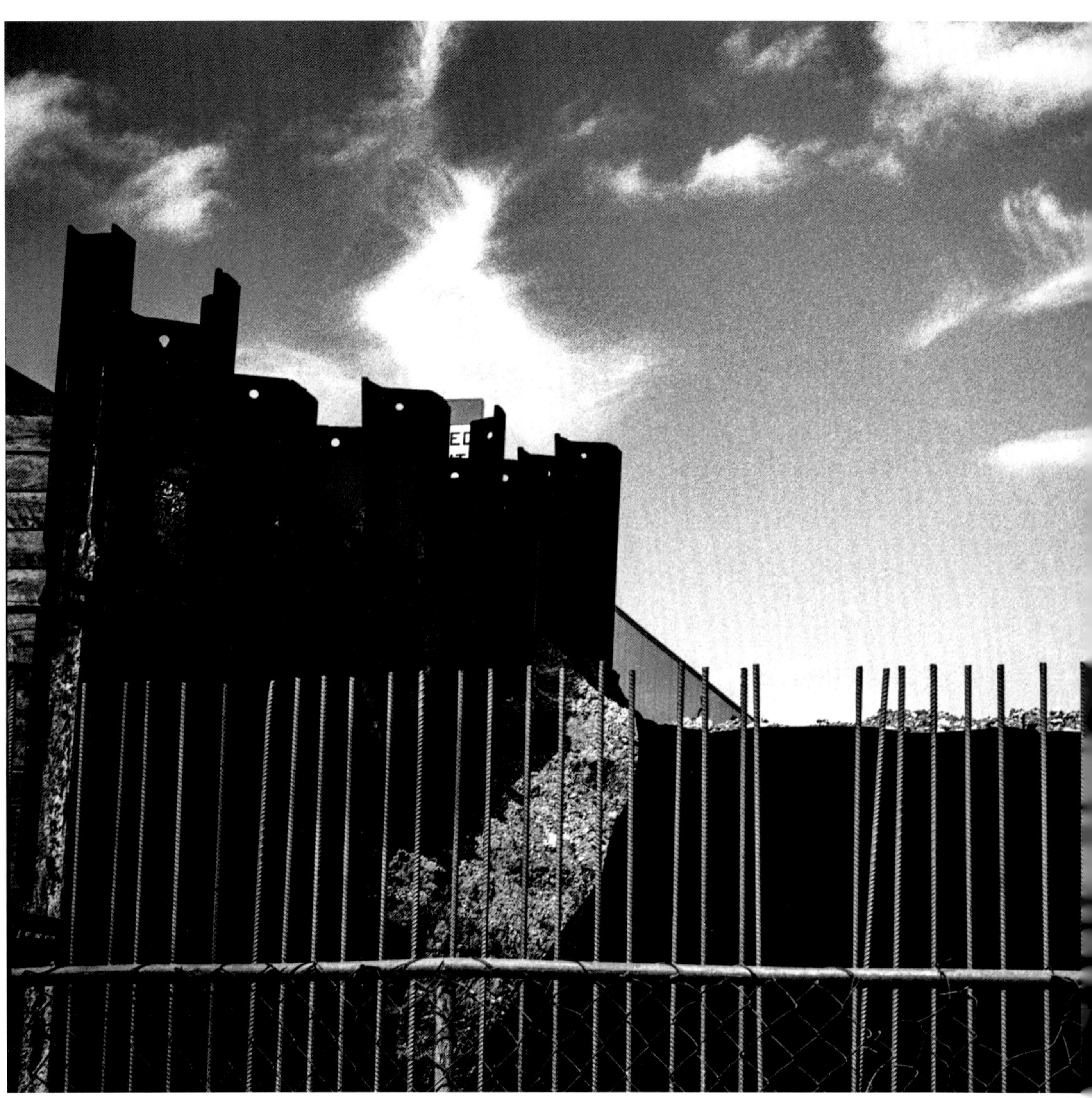

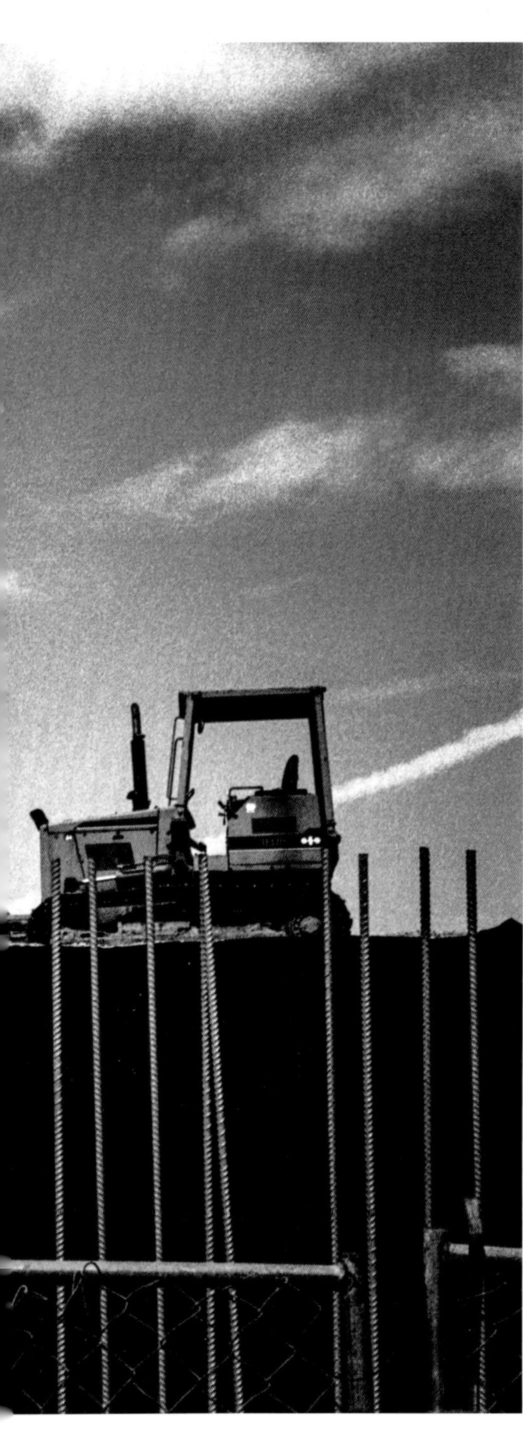

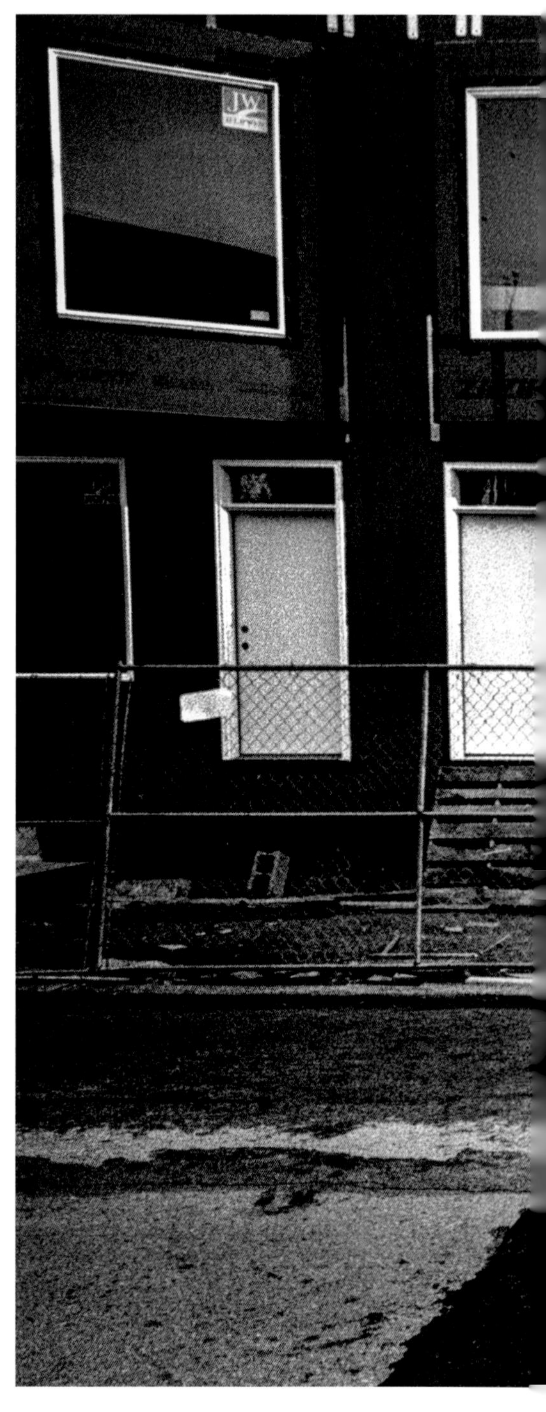

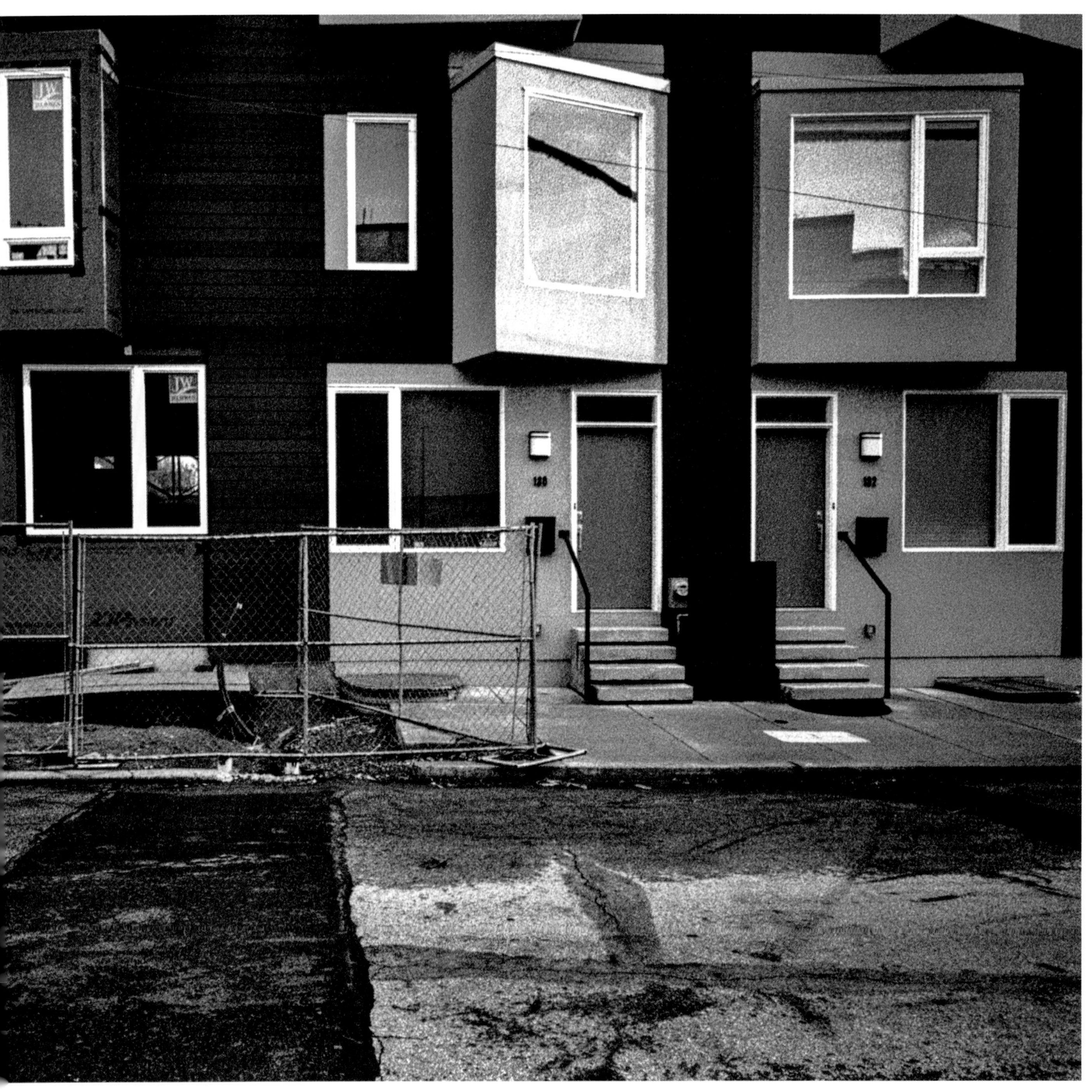

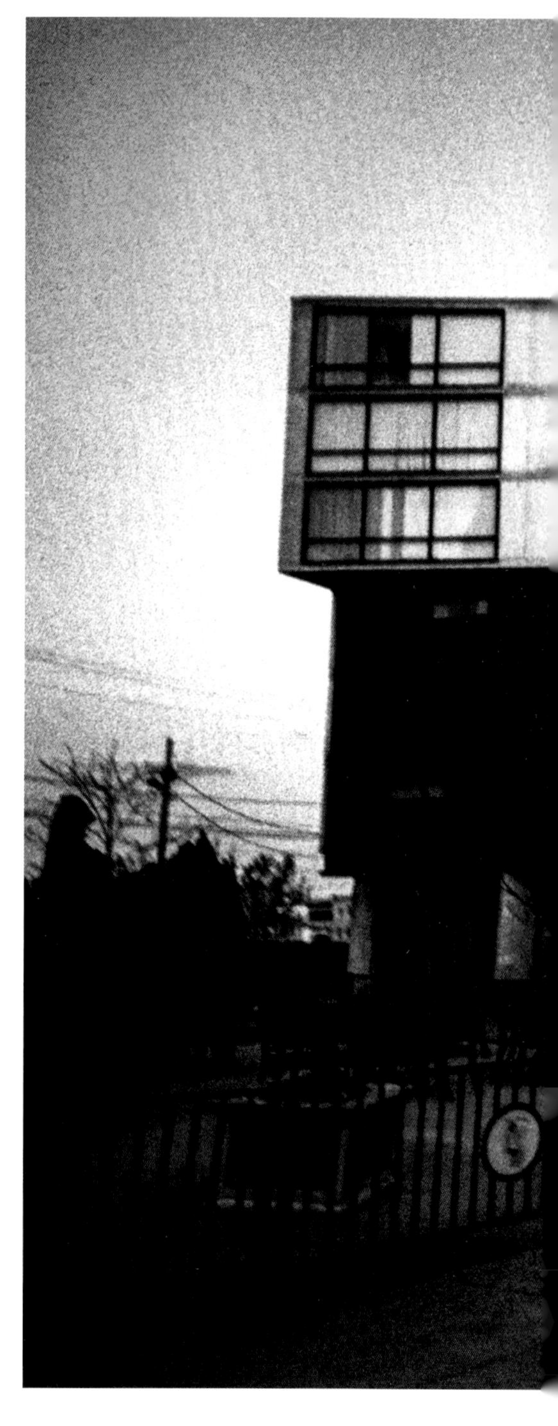

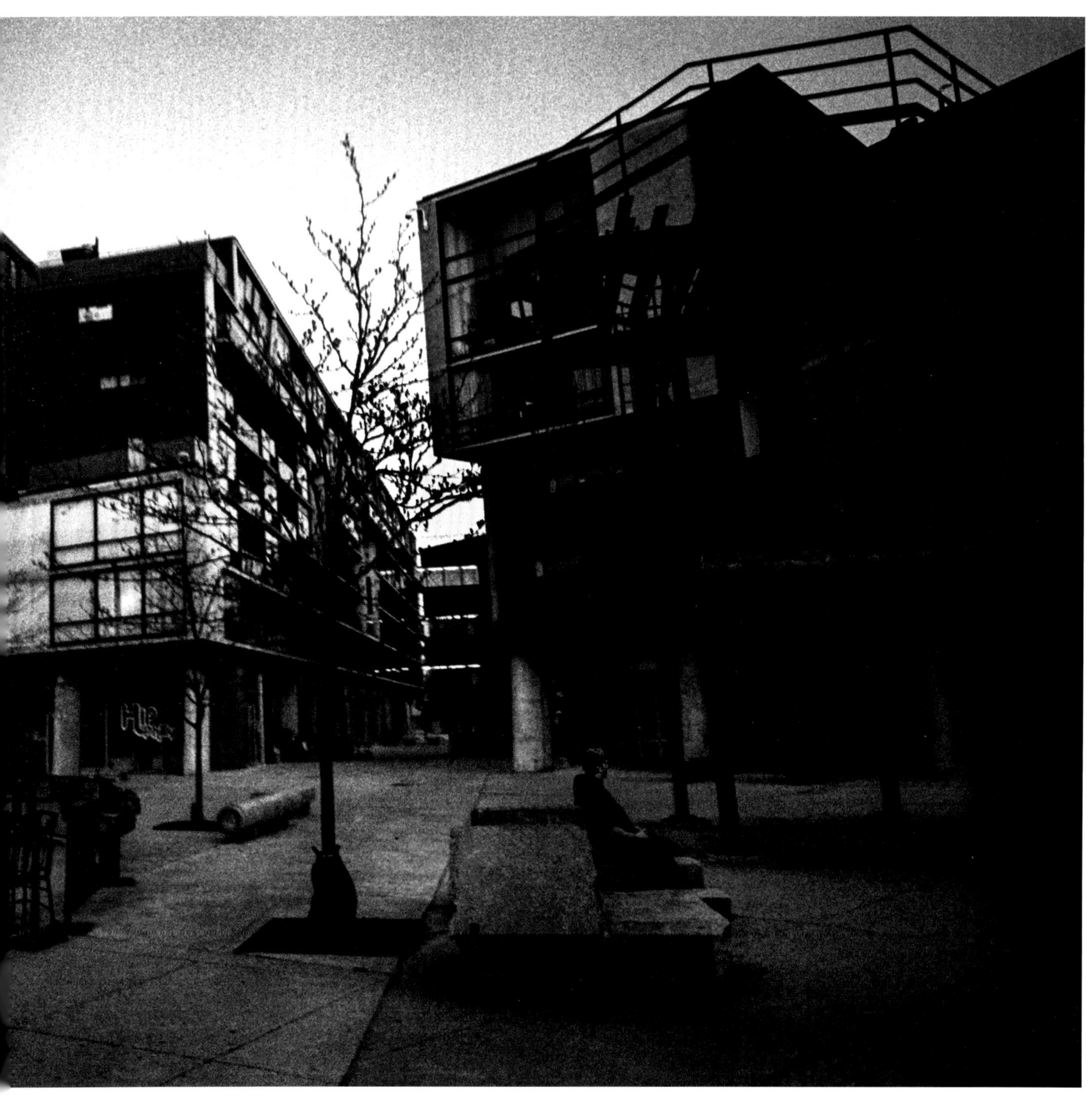

Platelist

Ghostly Traces: Wandering the Urban Interstices

The title of John Waller's photobook *Permanent Drift* is an allusion to French philosopher and Marxist theorist Guy Debord. More specifically it conjures Debord's idea of *le dérive* (literally "drift"), a radical practice for understanding, repurposing, resisting the way built environments are intended to be lived in, passed through, felt. Like Debord's practice, essentially a form of whimsical wandering, Waller's photos defamiliarize us to the borderlines between "somewheres" (obvious and intentional destinations—Center City, Philadelphia, for example, the skyline of which appears in the distance in more than one of these photographs) and "nowheres" (the interstitial places we tend to—and are intended to—ignore; the vacant and unused spaces now witnessing Philadelphia's transition from secondary city to moneyed paradise).

That's the spatial part, the physical "drift." But the title, and the images in the book, imply more. As with all photographs, in their seeming permanence lies another source of defamiliarization, concerning time. It's a contradiction Roland Barthes teases out in *Camera Lucida* when he muses over Alexander Gardner's 1865 photograph of Lewis Payne, the would-be assassin of Secretary of State W.H. Seward, as the handcuffed young man awaits execution. Of the photograph's subject, Barthes writes, "He is dead, and he is going to die." This is in keeping with the medium's unique disorientation. Photographs are about, simultaneously, both absence and presence—what *was* (in that a photograph is concrete residue of an irrefutable past) and what *still is* (the illusion-built-on-presence, which, like this book, you can hold in your hands). This contradiction lies at the core of the photographs in *Permanent Drift*. "Ghostly Traces" could be its subtitle.

I locate the spirit of Waller's work somewhere between my two other favorite Philadelphia photographers—Ray Metzker and Will Brown. Like Metzker, Waller has a strong eye for geometry, in the bold lines of the shifting architecture and in the city's omnipresent play of light and shadow. And yet Waller seems drawn to the same dramatic Tarkovskian texture that gives Brown's photos their coarse sensuality. Like these two predecessors, but unlike more conventional "street photographers," Waller's work seems less concerned with people as concrete presences with individual identities than with—that phrase again—the *ghostly traces* they leave. And as is often the case with Metzker, the individual identities of the few people we do encounter in Waller's book are effaced, blurred, obscured, forgotten.

That said, Waller's own intelligent presence suffuses these evocative photographs. The book is a layered diary, a travelogue of his wanderings—of his daily *dérives*—through and around the Philadelphia neighborhood where he lived for a number of years. That period coincided with an acceleration of Philadelphia's latter-day demographic changes—people with money moving back into the city—and of the resulting explosion in real estate development. During this time many of the city's architectural and cultural treasures were demolished to make way for sleek mid-century modern apartment buildings. Olde Kensington, where Waller lived, might be called an "interstitial" neighborhood. It's just north of the more celebrated Northern Liberties (so "young and hip") and just west of the infamous ("close-knit") Fishtown. The collection constitutes a mapping out of this neighborhood's *psychogeography*—or, more pointedly, of Waller's experience of that neighborhood. Another of Debord's conceptual legacies, psychogeography refers to what he calls the "specific effects of the geographical environment (whether consciously organized or not) on the emotions and behavior of individuals." And this sense of occupied space is precisely what emerges as one wanders through Waller's book. It's an accumulation of the concrete sensate and sensual experiences of what it was like to live there during that moment of change—and what it is like to live in the built environment, in the *unintended interstices*, of a major American urban center.

As we meander through the book, we begin to notice patterns and visual themes or concerns, or at least what draws Waller's keen eye again and again. There's a feeling of twilight in these photographs. Though only a few are literally taken at that time of day, night seems always to be falling. And everywhere, forces are afoot that seek, intentionally or not, to undermine the stark utilitarian purposes of the built environment and render it beautiful. Vines and opportunistic trees well up from weedy lots to overtake houses. Facades flake and crumble. Smoke stacks of decommissioned electrical plants rust in the distance. Refuse accumulates around ossifying technology. The edges of Tyvek-wrapped buildings flutter in the wind. Nameless people leave things behind—trophies, footballs, caution cones, tire tracks—where they molder, crimp, deflate, fill with rainwater. It's as if there's something moving through the landscape that refuses to be contained, a restless, half-articulated urge, like someone who cuts an "A" through a chain-link fence rather than walk around it, and in doing so creates a new, organic pathway to some unknowable destination. Everywhere we encounter the inscrutable: cryptic messages and effaced signifiers, blank billboards, illegible scrawl and faded graffiti, a shroud of snow that resolves itself into a teddy bear lashed to a metal fence post. And over everything, the omnipresent shadow stencils—even more fleeting—designs approaching the abstract, diagonals on scored concrete walls, the crisscross of scaffolding, the configurations of pigeons arrested in curved flight.

Waller's time in Olde Kensington was itself interstitial. It has ended. He has since moved north, back to western Massachusetts, where he grew up. It is in this more bucolic setting that he edited these photographs, the photobook finding, as Wordsworth writes of the poetic process, "its origin from emotion recollected in tranquility." It seems in keeping with my own experience of urban spaces that Waller had to leave the city, with its unrelenting distractions, in order to truly see it. The result? *Permanent Drift*, like the work of many other accomplished photographers, pulls back the veil that daily living drapes over our vision to reveal what James Agee, in another remarkable photobook, calls "the cruel radiance of what is." I am grateful for the gift of this volume.

—Pete Duval

Acknowledgments

This book is dedicated to my friends and family.

Jeanette, without your enduring love and support, none of this would be possible.

Thanks to Ben Marrs and Rick Myers. Special thanks to Jordan Baumgarten for his generous feedback and mentorship, and to Tsuyoshi Ito, who provided a vital place for photographic education in the old neighborhood; I'll never forget the lessons each of you have taught me. To Pete Duval for his insightful writing and thoughtful conversations; I look forward to more.

Thanks to everyone at Daylight Books for their hard work in bringing this book to print.